THE

OLD-TIME SALOON

The Old-Time Saloon was originally published in 1931, eleven years into Prohibition, which lasted from 1920 until 1933. This facsimile includes a new introduction, explanatory notes at the back, and a bibliography.

This edition is published for a
Chosen Few who will Understand.
The spot to the left is a Tear Drop.

George Ade

MM 10-1931

No. 467

Rea Irvin

"Thanks—I jest et.
I'll have a cigar."

THE
OLD-TIME SALOON

NOT WET — NOT DRY

JUST HISTORY

GEORGE ADE

INTRODUCED AND ANNOTATED BY
BILL SAVAGE

The University of Chicago Press
Chicago and London

The University of Chicago Press, Chicago 60637
The University of Chicago Press, Ltd., London
Introduction, Notes, and Bibliography © 2016 by
    The University of Chicago
First published in 1931 by Ray Long & Richard R. Smith
University of Chicago Press edition 2016
Printed in the United States of America

25 24 23 22 21 20 19 18 17 16   1 2 3 4 5

ISBN-13: 978-0-226-41230-6   (paper)
ISBN-13: 978-0-226-41244-3   (e-book)
DOI: 10.7208/chicago/9780226412443.001.0001

Library of Congress Cataloging-in-Publication Data

Names: Ade, George, 1866–1944, author. | Savage, Bill, editor.
Title: The old-time saloon : not wet, not dry, just history / George
    Ade ; introduced and annotated by Bill Savage.
Description: Chicago ; London : The University of Chicago Press,
    2016. | Originally published: New York : R. Long & R.R. Smith,
    1931.
Identifiers: LCCN 2016017247 | ISBN 9780226412306 (pbk. : alk.
    paper) | ISBN 9780226412443 (e-book)
Subjects: LCSH: Bars (Drinking establishments)—United States. |
    Drinking of alcoholic beverages—United States.
Classification: LCC TX947 .A3 2016 | DDC 647.9573—dc23
    LC record available at https://lccn.loc.gov/2016017247

♾ This paper meets the requirements of ANSI/NISO Z39.48-1992
(Permanence of Paper).

INTRODUCTION

George Ade was once one of the most famous writers in America.

Indiana native and Purdue University graduate, he came to Chicago in 1891, where he made his name as a reporter covering disasters, boxing matches, and the 1893 World's Columbian Exposition. Readers ate up his work, so wise editors gave him freedom to write pretty much whatever he wanted. His columns for the *Chicago Record*—Stories of the Streets and of the Town, and Fables in Slang—were nationally syndicated and then collected into best-selling books. By 1904, he became the first playwright to have three plays on Broadway simultaneously: the now-forgotten Gilbert-and-Sullivan-esque comedies *The Sultan of Sulu*, *The County Chairman*, and *The College Widow*. In the early days of film, he directed several short movies and wrote scripts or stories for over a hundred more. After financial success enabled him to retire altogether, he continued to write essays and the occasional Fable for national magazines from his Indiana estate or his winter home in Miami.

Ade combined a pitch-perfect ear for common speech

with insight into the humor of everyday life. Like the American writer he most admired, Mark Twain, Ade captured the way people actually spoke. As a journalist, he relentlessly sought out material in the main streets and back alleys of Chicago, producing long stories daily that were often illustrated by cartoonist John McCutcheon. This urban exploration meant spending no small amount of time in Chicago's countless saloons, vital places which played a central role in the life of the city beyond just providing drinks, as free lunches fed factory workers and politicians huddled in their beery headquarters.

In this volume, Ade brings his comic sensibility to bear on the pre-Prohibition saloon. This peculiarly American drinking establishment was not exactly the same thing as a pub, a tavern, or an inn, and its very popularity, from roughly 1870 to 1920, helped to bring about its demise. In 1931, most Americans (due to their age, gender, politics, or religion) would never have set foot in a saloon. In the context of arguments for the repeal of Prohibition, Ade pretends to simply remind his readers of what the joints were like—the bartenders and the regulars, the sporting art on the walls, and the sentimental sing-alongs. He explores the economics of saloons in small towns and big cities and explains why bootleggers get filthy rich. Ade freely admits that the saloon earned its fate because competition led to abuses of social propriety, not to mention the law. He is objective and pulls few punches.

But in his heart, Ade's got one foot on the brass rail, a cold-cut sandwich from the free lunch in his hand, and a gentleman's pour of whiskey, with a snit of beer as a chaser, on the counter in front of him.

Just as Ade hoped to inspire his readers with nostalgia, the goal of this new edition of *The Old-Time Saloon* is to take twenty-first-century readers back to the debate over the repeal of Prohibition and to the saloon culture which Drys demonized. Notes appended to the book provide details about the politics, personalities, and everyday saloon life Ade depicts, from the long-forgotten Anti-Saloon League to an inventor of stand-up comedy to the traditional recipes for several cocktails. The notes also dig deeper into the relationship between the saloon, entertainment culture, and vice, as well as the complex gender politics of what was once an almost exclusively masculine part of the American landscape.

This new edition seems especially appropriate at this moment in American history. As writers about the relationship between alcohol and American culture inevitably note, the pendulum swings. From Colonial days onward, America was the heaviest-drinking country in the world. Then alcohol was outlawed altogether. Then Prohibition was repealed. After the repeal, American drinking culture was dominated for decades by a few national brands of beer, wine, and spirits, but now small breweries, vineyards, and distillers flourish. As of November 2015, America had the greatest number of licensed breweries in its history: 4,144 (13 more than the former high-suds mark, in 1873, before the growth of mega-breweries in St. Louis and Milwaukee). Now, in big cities and small towns, bars featuring craft beers and elaborate artisanal cocktails hearken back to the world of saloons that Prohibition almost, but not quite, obliterated.

Ade knew that saloon culture intimately, from the proper technique for mixing a drink (twirled with a long-handled spoon, not shaken—the cocktail shaker being a Prohibition-era import from the UK; see pp. 51–52) to the infallible judgment of bouncers tossing out over-served or free-lunch freeloaders (p. 41) and the generous wit of a bartender whom you could reliably just call Mike or Otto or Bill (p. 96). With this new edition, I hope to bring the old-time saloon back to life in some small way, to enlighten our view of American history, and perhaps to enrich our contemporary culture of public drinking as well.

Bill Savage
Chicago, 2016

CONTENTS

ILLUSTRATIONS

THE SNAKE

BACK in the days of deep tan and stone-bruises we boys knew that when we killed a garter snake, the animal might be as dead as a door-nail, but the tail would continue to writhe and squirm and wiggle until sundown. This is going to be an apt comparison, because the serious cartoonists of the church and anti-whisky publications, during the long drive against red liquor, always pictured Alcoholic Drink as a coiled serpent with fangs as long as from here to there. Nearly a dozen years ago the Anti-Saloon League, the W. C. T. U., the white neck-tie preachers and all of those deacons who never drank anything stronger than Hostetter's Bitters, closed in on the enemy. They pounded Mr. Snake with stones and battered him with clubs until he was just a battered and unrecognizable smear. They looked at the mangled remains and said: "Well, that job's done! Now there isn't an evil influence left in the world."

One of the rejoicing editorial writers used an unfortunate expression in recording the victory. He said that the forces of righteousness had "scotched the serpent." He forgot that there are two definitions for "scotch." It may mean "to put an end to." Or, it may mean something that costs $80 a case and never was within three thousand miles of Aberdeen.

We all know that the venomous thing was killed in 1920, but the tail is still seemingly alive and slapping around in all directions. No one will dispute that statement and, least of all, the good people who are dead set against the drink habit. They are still attacking the whitened skeleton of the retail liquor traffic because the tail continues to wiggle. They are denouncing the saloon as if we still had one on every corner. They just can't believe that the vicious old reptile is really dead as long as that tail keeps on writhing and squirming. When death agonies continue over a period of ten years, that's a record!

The trouble nowadays is that hardly any one can write about distilled, vinous and malt beverages without trying to float a lot of propaganda. All who write or speak for or against the occasional hoisting of the hip flask or the sharp rattle of ice in the shaker seem to be fighting mad. They become so overheated from using mean adjectives that they can't calm down and discuss the past, present and future of the Prohibition Crusade and the brewery output and the conversion of corn into corn juice without getting into a lather and abusing the opposition.

Is it possible to talk about various beverages containing more than one-half of one percent of kick, to ponder upon the causes leading up to Prohibition and to give some information regarding the old-time saloon without taking sides or circulating propaganda? Undoubtedly.

In the succeeding pages dealing with retail establishments which sold intoxicating fluids under sanction of the law, nothing will be said or done with the intent of giving offense to the extreme Drys or the extreme Wets or that in-between population which may be classed as Slightly Moist. The idea is to dish up history instead of attempting to influence legislation. The record of the bar-room and the influences behind it may be read aloud from any Baptist

3

pulpit without arousing a protest from any member of the flock. Not much will be written about the effects of the 18th Amendment and the Volstead Act and no remedies will be proposed. Enough has been said and is being said and will be said without any brash volunteers rushing into the controversy. Just for the sake of novelty, we are going to join friendly hands and stroll into the past and find out what all the shooting is about by reminding ourselves of some undeniable facts concerning a certain kind of public resort called a "saloon."

No use talking, any viper that looks like a boa constrictor ten years after it is extinct, is worth talking about. Furthermore, they *are* talking about it. Those who insist upon continuing the noble experiment say: "If we compromise with the law-breakers and the forces of evil, it means a return of the saloon and its whole train of attendant horrors." Every militant Wet and member of the Association Against the Whole Proposition is shouting at the top of his voice: "Listen! We are opposed to the saloon, the same as you are. All we want is something to drink at a reasonable price and with the quality guaranteed."

4

The snake may continue to wiggle the tail, but no one has a friendly word for the snake. If you care to investigate you may discover evidences of the wiggle in any speak-easy and at many soft-drink parlors, table d'hote restaurants, road-houses, filling stations, barbecue stands and, possibly, a few hardware stores. But, even the obliging benefactor who is willing to slip you, for seventy-five cents, a shot of something that looks like kerosene and smells like arnica, will tell you that the saloon was an evil influence and we are a darn sight better off without it. All knocking it but still talking about it.

Do you recall any prominent and honored citizen of your neighborhood who passed on in 1920 and who is still a topic of daily conversation in the houses up and down your street? He is as much in the past tense as Julius Cæsar. But the scaly orthopoid monster known as the Saloon Business is still receiving obituary notices. As a member of the animal kingdom he must have been something of a dangerous reptile or he would not be remembered so vividly or hated so bitterly.

2

DISCUSSING
WICKEDNESS

HOW many of you can claim any real knowledge of the saloon, obtained at first hand?

If the author let's on to know a good deal about the places at which drinkables were dispensed in the olden days, it is because every kind of saloon came under his observation. An explanation is inserted here and now to head off any sarcastic reader who might suggest that the title of this work should be "Confessions of an Ill-Spent Life."

He put in his boyhood and youth in a prairie town that had one watch-repairer, one druggist, one blacksmith and four saloons. He was not permitted to enter these dens of vice but he could not avoid smelling them or hearing the songs and the babble of loud and foolish talk. The street fights between a couple of agricultural huskies who had trained on copper-distilled Kentucky Sour Mash was a free show and the parade which trailed behind the

Town Marshal and the combative drunk, up Main Street toward the "calaboose," was a frequent spectacle, not without educational value.

He was in a college town for six years. The population was 20,000 and there were exactly 94 saloons in full blast, most of them ignoring laws intended to regulate the opening and closing hours and prohibit any sale to minors. Any one tall enough to hook his chin over the dispensing counter could obtain for a nickel a large goblet of beer. The goblet could have been used as an aquarium for gold-fish. The period was the eighties and "keg parties" were popular. Usually they were held out in the woods, and the large, perspiring keg was surrounded by "weenies," pretzels and young men who were preparing themselves to face the stern responsibilities of life.

From 1890 to 1900 the collector of the ensuing historical data was a hard-working newspaper slave in Chicago. For three years he did assorted reporting and for seven years he handled a two-column department known as Stories of the Streets and of the Town. He had to and he did snoop the wicked city from one end to the other. The Chicago of the nineties

7

had nothing to learn from Port Said, Singapore, the lake front at Buffalo, the sea front at Bombay, or the crib section of New Orleans—the aforesaid spots having a world-wide reputation for wild wickedness. Chicago was just as tough as it knew how to be, and that's as much as you can ask of any town. Saloons everywhere and many of them open all night and all day Sunday. One of the most familiar statements in playful circulation was to the effect that when a drink parlor was opened anywhere in the loop, the proprietor went over and threw the key into the lake. The more famous hang-outs had not been closed for a single minute for years and years.

A blaring and glaring and insolent red-light district held day and night revelry on the very rim of the most highly respectable business section. Everything went, from pitch-and-toss to manslaughter. One could get into a poolroom or gambling house just as easily as he could get into the Public Library. The sea-going hacks rested all day and rattled all night. Thieves were protected and opium joints were benignly regarded as public necessities. If any member of a gang was caught in the drag net

8

IN
CONFERENCE

Courtesy of *Cosmopolitan*

and slammed into the hoosegow, an alderman always appeared in the police court to secure his release.

How often did I hear the same old plea: "Your Honor, I've known this boy for years. He's a good boy an' works hard an' takes care of his ole mother. Mebbe he'd been drinkin' a little beer an' fell in with a hard crowd, but—"

The "boy" would be standing there, a perfect specimen of beetle-browed thug, with a record for house-breaking, vandalism, pandering and murderous assault.

The court was always merciful, for the reason that the alderman making the plea was one of several aldermen who had secured his appointment as police magistrate.

Probably no other city on earth ever got as much bad publicity as Chicago has received in the last ten years. Approximately 500 gangsters have been "bumped off" and the grand total of bribe money handed to officials would settle all of the European war-debt problems. We all know about the killings, but if the general public ever got the low-down and inside information on the number of officials who have been bought up and how much they took into the open hand, then Chicago would get some more press-agenting of the kind it doesn't need on the eve of the great Exposition.

Because I knew Chicago so well during the rampageous wide-open period and have kept close tab on recent developments through certain residents who know how to operate the X-Ray, I cannot refrain from drawing comparisons. Chicago was undeniably wicked in the nineties and it has been accused of dreadful wickedness during the twenties and into the early thirties. Our old friend, the snake with the ugly fangs, was chief organizer of the cussedness about forty years ago and he is said to have been in full partnership with Al Capone and his grim crew during the last ten years, and, because we are trying to write a fair biography of this same serpent, it will be proper to set down the differences between two kinds of outlawry.

During the nineties all of the alluring vices flaunted themselves in the open. Satan had all of his merchandise in the show-windows. The managers of the prolonged carnival did not kill one another. They co-operated, in the most friendly manner, to get rich by playing on the

12

weaknesses of those who had lustful appetites and who were just as short on scruples as they were long on thirst. Just one big happy family.

The saloon of the nineties was denounced as a nesting-place for fraudulent voters, political crooks, lazy vags, organized criminals, cheap gamblers and painted females who strolled along all of the busy streets trying to become acquainted with men who had not yet learned about the badger game or the use of chloral hydrate as a sure producer of sound and prolonged sleep.

What a town it was! A certain greenie from the country observed this modern combination of Sodom and Gomorrah and supposed that all other big cities in the United States were about the same. A good many of them were.

All of the head-line attractions of that old-time sinful saturnalia have been wiped out. The day-and-night saloon is merely a memory. The red-light district was moved two miles to the south and later it was erased from the map. The lower courts are now ruled by able judges who cannot be touched by corrupt influences. Open gambling houses, open pool-rooms and convenient hop-joints are not tolerated. The

13

lodging-house hoboes are no longer wintered by the thousands in order to carry elections. Stately sky-scrapers have been erected upon the sites of reeking doggeries and cigar store fronts masking unspeakable orgies. The lake front park, where an army of shabby derelicts used to sprawl every warm night, like the strewn dead on a battle-field, is one of the beauty spots of the world.

Once in a while I go in from the country to look at the city I knew so well and which befriended me and opened the door of opportunity. The frontier metropolis with which I hob-nobbed has disappeared. In its stead has arisen a new city of Titanic towers, gorgeous architecture, amazing stretches of immaculate boulevards, overwhelming vistas, and a thousand tributes to beauty instead of a thousand tributes to gross materialism, tinctured with gaudy vice.

Going back as a Rip Van Winkle, I can motor all around town without discovering one trace of the glaring sinfulness which gave Chicago such an evil reputation in the nineties. When I was a reporter I heard a lot of shooting and once I discovered the body of a mur-

14

dered man just across the street from our
rooming-house, and when John McCutcheon
and I walked south on Wabash Avenue late at
night to get to our humble nook at Peck Court
and Michigan Avenue, we used the middle of
the street, so that no hold-up man could step
out from an alley and salute us with a piece
of lead covered with leather (professionally
known as a "black-jack") or an elongated
canvas bag filled with sand. If he had robbed
us, the joke would have been on him but, just
the same, we didn't want to have our heads
caved in. Finally we moved over to the north
side and took refuge among the law-abiding
Germans.

The whole present situation is most confus-
ing to some of us who knew the old rip-snort-
ing and ruffianly Chicago and now find a
brand-new metropolis which strikes us as being
a combination of the Garden of Eden and the
Grand Canyon of the Colorado. As often as
I have gone back, I never have seen any one
who looked like a Sicilian shooting at some one
else who, also, looked like a Sicilian. They say
that whole fleets of beer-trucks move from one
place to another, guarded by policemen, but I

never have discovered one of the trucks. They say there are night dancing places and shuttered speak-easies where one may sneak in, having secured credentials, and buy cocktails that smell something like cocktails, at a mere dollar a piece. Maybe these drink-parlors are operating but I never saw the inside of one and I never will, unless some one blindfolds me and backs me in. Not that I am unfamiliar with the sight of some one demonstrating his disapproval of the 18th Amendment. But, why go to a lot of trouble in order to be gypped?

Pardon this long detour but we cannot intelligently investigate the wiggle of the snake's tail unless we regard conditions in some such place where, outwardly, everything seems cleansed and purified while inwardly, if we are to believe the newspapers, life is just one high jinks after another with nothing to mar the festivities except the occasional carrying out of the dead.

Once I was supposed to be a fairly keen reporter but now I must be asleep at the switch. If I hadn't read all the books about gangsters and all the articles about oceans of beer and Niagaras of synthetic hooch, I would

16

be under the impression that the old town had
gone pretty much Presbyterian except for ten
thousand parties in private apartments and
select homes, or secluded trysting places where
open-minded collegians and liberated flappers
are wont to "play around" together. Probably
no one past the age of fifty can quite fathom
the significance of this modern "playing
around." It seems to mean that any young
person can do anything as long as violations
of the statutes and fractures of the moral law
are perpetrated in a spirit of fun and not in
earnest. Stop me, if I am wrong.

The old-trade-marks of alcoholic hilarity
have vanished but the would-be repealers insist
that we have generated conditions which are
more disgraceful and more dangerous than
those of the decades immediately preceding the
World War. The confirmed Drys insist that
nothing that can happen under Prohibition
will stack up along side of the multiplied horrors of the Dark Ages when saloons were
running. Whichever side is right, people should
be informed about saloons, bar-keeps, free
lunches and the continued desire of our citi-
zenry to rest their feet on the brass rail.

17

WHAT WAS A SALOON —
AND WHY?

IF you think there is no call for the work now under way, consider a few facts. You know that the Anti-Saloon League, the W. C. T. U., and other societies specializing on moral welfare are still fighting the saloon. What do the residents of our fair, or fair to middling, land know about the saloon, what it looked like, what it smelled like, what it sold and to whom, and why it became such a peril and nuisance that years after being legally wiped out of existence it is still regarded as a menace?

Half of the territory of the United States was Sahara dry under local option forty years ago. More than half of the states were dry by legislative enactments twenty-five years ago. All of the public drinking places were restricted during the War Period and the Government measures wiping out every saloon on the map went into effect eleven years ago.

Stop and count up. Even in the cities which are now regarded as Anti-Prohibition strongholds, no person under the age of thirty-two ever saw the inside of a saloon. Young men and young women attaining their majorities this year have dim recollections of lager beer signs and bottles lined up behind plate glass fronts. No one under fifteen can distinctly recall seeing a grog shop, a distillery, or a brewery in open and unashamed operation. To them the "family resort" is just as much ancient history as the Battle of Bunker Hill or the Fall of the Bastille.

Furthermore, taking into account the fact that very few women who date back to the old wide-open days ever visited a saloon, and that residents of many states have to be at least fifty years of age in order to cherish any definite recollections of hardwood bars and foaming faucets, and that a large slice of the population, even during the high tide of the wet era, shunned the booze joints and rode on the wagon or partook politely in clubs, hotels or restaurants, and you are compelled to admit that probably three-fourths of the population of our land are densely ignorant regarding the

19

bar-rooms which swarmed so insolently during the Victorian period. Yet, the saloon is a live issue eleven years after the liquor traffic was laid out in a casket and formally dispatched to the cemetery.

As we look back at those old days, when every shifting breeze of a city street was laden with a malty aroma and any kind of drink was procurable at your own price, it becomes more and more evident that the U. S. A. went dry because the distillers, the brewers and the retail dealers in wines, liquors and cigars were a lot of overbearing and impudent dumbbells. Even when the supreme catastrophe hovered over them, they were not bright enough to recognize the fact that disaster was impending and that they were about to take a long ride. They had made a joke of the law and flouted the pious element and worked in cahoots with low-browed politicians so long that they believed themselves immune from any sort of interference. Their record was so unsavory that when the 18th Amendment and the Volstead Act were being put across by the astute Mr. Wayne B. Wheeler, thousands and thousands of voters who believed with Wood-

Courtesy of *Cosmopolitan*   Gluyas Williams

SNEAKING IN

row Wilson that the Constitution of the United States was not framed for the purpose of regulating social habits, remained in the background and preserved silence because they could not become actively Wet without seeming to be in partnership with a lot of boys who had been misbehaving themselves.

The trouble with the drink places was that they tried to think up cute ways of making a fool of the law instead of wisely endeavoring to keep up a semblance of decency and placate the non-customers. In communities which attempted to enforce midnight closing they went in for double curtains and heavy blinds, so that when the place seemed dark from the outside it was very much illuminated and going full blast on the inside. Keeping open on Sundays and holidays, selling to minors, harboring outlaw elements, lining up voters who could be bought—these were some of the major offenses. Do you remember the Raines Law? It was passed by the New York legislature late in the last century and was intended to close all saloons on Sunday. Mr. William Raines worked out a very hard-boiled enactment which provided awful punishment for any retailer who passed stuff over the bar on the Sabbath Day. The law made an exception in favor of hotels, permitting them to serve drinks to their guests on Sunday, *provided* that the guests received their liquid nourishment in conjunction with food regularly and properly set out on the table. Yes, indeed! So every saloon in New York City became a hotel. It set up a couple of cots and kept a fake register behind the bar and the customers had to sit around a table with a "prop" sandwich on it and go as far as they liked, with the understanding that no one should disturb the sandwich. Any place that was raided could produce witnesses to prove that the joint was really an honest-to-goodness hostelry, with a register for guests, and at least one bedroom, and that no drinks were served except to patrons who sat at tables with food in front of them. What is more, they got away with it— for a while. More plain history, not intended to influence the electorate, one way or another.

One purpose of this book is to give candid facts regarding the average saloon and explain why it became unpopular. Also, an attempt will be made to tell of the ruthless methods

24

employed by the organized distillers and brewers and their agents, the retail dealers, too many of whom were in partnership with habitual criminals, conniving politicians, and chalk-white ladies who wore their sailor hats down over their eyes.

The distillers were to blame because they consistently refused to make concessions to a populace which became more and more indignant over the manner in which the drink problem was being avoided instead of being solved. The brewers were in wrong because they took over virtual ownership of a large percentage of saloons and compelled the managers of drinking places to resort to every kind of vulgar device to promote sales and operate at a profit. The landlords and barkeeps invited trouble for themselves by ignoring the law and victimizing customers by passing out cheap grades of liquid stimulant and working all sorts of dubious schemes to get easy money. In other words, the flat-heads who were attempting to handle a ticklish situation showed all the diplomatic subtlety of mud turtles. Possibly we may condense the whole situation of 1920 into the following statement:

25

THE NON-DRINKERS HAD BEEN ORGANIZING FOR FIFTY YEARS AND THE DRINKERS HAD NO OR-GANIZATION WHATEVER. They had been too busy, drinking.

Why did the saloon get such a bad name? Bishop Potter said it was "the poor man's club." To many a weak mortal it was an oasis of good cheer in a desert of sordid business activities. Not all of the proprietors were villains and it is a matter of history that nearly every bar-keep had to be guide, counselor, friend and sympathetic listener to any gentleman, being buffeted by Fate, who wished to stay up until about midnight and have a good cry.

The truth is that the average or typical saloon was not a savory resort. The old Hoffman House bar, home of the Manhattan cocktail, with ten thousand dollar paintings on the walls and "Ed" Stokes circulating amiably among the important customers, was quite unlike the low-browed shack on the outskirts of a big steel mill with the half-naked puddlers coming in to gulp down enormous hookers of straight rye, each heroic wallop being followed by a tall glass of beer as a "chaser."

The famous Knickerbocker drinking parlor with Old King Cole by Maxfield Parrish beaming down on the convivial members of "The Forty-Second Street Country Club," was not related to the small-town dump where the hard nuts from the farming districts assembled to get themselves liquored "to the key-hole" and then pull off rough-and-tumble fights, rolling around in the saw-dust.

When we say "saloon," we are not referring to such gilt-edge and exceptional places as the Sazerac or Ramos in New Orleans, or the splendiferous Righeimer's in Chicago, or the Planters' or Tony Faust's in St. Louis, or the Antlers in San Antonio, or the Palace in San Francisco or the mint-julep headquarters in the old White at White Sulphur Springs, or the busy Waldorf in New York or the much frequented Touraine in Boston. Every city had at least one expensively decorated "buffet" where the socially elect could become pickled under polite auspices. For every one of the *de luxe* establishments there were a thousand boozing kens all of the same conventional

27

pattern and specializing on a few standardized beverages instead of featuring fancy mahogany fixtures and elaborate free lunches served by menials in spotless white. Nine-tenths of all the places in which intoxicants were dished out affected a splendor which was palpably spurious and made a total failure of any attempt to seem respectable. The saloon business was furtive and ashamed of itself, hiding behind curtains, blinds and screens and providing alley entrances for those who wished to slip in without being observed.

When you had visited one of the old-time saloons you had seen a thousand. Very often it stood on a corner so as to have two street entrances and wave a gilded beer sign at pedestrians drifting along from any point of the compass. The entrance was through swinging doors which were shuttered so that any one standing on the outside could not see what was happening on the inside. The windows were masked by grille work, potted ferns, one-sheet posters and a fly-specked array of fancy-shaped bottles which were merely symbols and not merchandise.

The bar counter ran lengthwise at one side

Courtesy of *Colliers*

THE BUNG-STARTER

of the dim interior and always had a brass foot-rail in front of it. Saw-dust on the floor was supposed to absorb the drippings. Behind the bar was a mirror and below the mirror a tasteful medley of lemons, assorted glasses and containers brightly labeled to advertise champagne, muscatel, port, sweet Catawba, sauterne and that sovereign remedy for bad colds, Rock and Rye. Most of these ornamental trimmings were aging in glass and there was no demand for them whatsoever. It was just one of the traditions of the trade that when a retailer received a license to sell "wines and liquors" he was supposed to have an array of grape beverages behind the bar to prove that he dealt in lady-like table wines as well as in forty-rod T.N.T. guaranteed to blow the hat off. The vine-yard products were supposed to give a tinge of aristocracy to a business venture which was otherwise terribly short on social standing. A feeble attempt was being made to suggest that some of the regulars drank claret. It would have poisoned them.

We come to mural decorations. One large chromo reproduction of a disrobed siren reclining on a couch. She was over-weight. But we are dealing with an era during which stream lines would have been a crime. The footlight favorites were shaped like bass viols. One evening at a club in Louisville a Colonel was describing the most beautiful girl in Kentucky. He said you could span her waist with your two hands but she couldn't sit down in a tub.

Prize fighters were featured in the pictorial adornments. Along about 1890 probably nine-tenths of the thirst parlors advertised John L. Sullivan, of the knobby biceps and curling moustache. He was idolized as a man-killer and also because he was the ideal customer. He slapped a large bill on the counter and called up the house and often tried to slug the bartender who pushed any change back to him. A man's man! That was long before the Boston Strong Boy ran away from the hard stuff and began to deliver temperance lectures.

Two of the favorite placards were: "Don't ask for credit," and "If drinking interferes with your business, cut out business." The colored prints were intended to keep alive the salty humor of Rabelais and often had to do with an accidental display of the female leg. They were supposed to be spicy but, later on, they wouldn't have caused a tremor in any sorority house.

Sometimes there was a pool table, always in a bad state of repair. When William S. Gilbert in his matchless libretto of "The Mikado" told of making the punishment fit the crime by compelling the billiard sharp to play extravagant matches on "a cloth untrue, with a twisted cue and elliptical billiard balls," he came very near describing the pocket game as played by the merry souses in the good old saloon days.

4

THE FREE LUNCH

NOW we come to a subject regarding which many illusions need to be dispelled. Meaning, of course, the free lunch. No doubt you have come across the legend that during the Golden Age of King Alcohol any willing buyer in any saloon could get for absolutely nothing all of the important food items for which Delmonico and Sherry charged large prices.

It is true that in any of the larger and more popular and prosperous drinking resorts with cathedral architecture and all the mixers wearing lodge emblems, the long table across from the bar showed a tempting variety of good things to eat. There might be salted nuts, roast turkey, a spiced ham, a few ribs of beef, potato salad, potato chips, ripe olives, sandwiches, Herkhimer County cheese, summer sausage and napkins. The colored boy in the white apron would slice off anything the customer seemed to crave and pile up a grand variety on a plate, especially if his palm had been crossed with silver. The seemingly boundless generosity of a few of the money-making emporiums is still talked about and happy memories of a sentimental character linger with the more elderly soaks who now submit to the extortions of the speak-easy.

Other bars not so generous would offer free bowls of soup every noon. Many would have free-lunch specialties for every day in the week, as, for instance: Monday, hot frankfurters; Tuesday, roast pork; Wednesday, roast mutton; Thursday, Irish stew; Friday, baked fish and dressing; Saturday, roast beef and mashed potatoes; Sunday, dry crackers. Many were wide open on the Sabbath day and others merely had the curtains down and the side entrance unlocked, but there seemed to be a general understanding that patrons would eat at home on the day of rest, which wasn't always so restful if enough of the gang got together.

Any open-hearted benefactor who began the practice of giving away liberal portions of food to his friends and customers was invariably annoyed by visits from undesirables pretending to be friends and also by ravages on

the free-lunch counter by low-down deceivers
who had not passed any money over the bar.
The code governing the privileges of the free-
lunch department was exacting and was observed by the genteel trade even if ignored by
tourists, who happened to be passing through
the city on foot, and other unfortunates who
had hit the grit. Hunger will overcome mod-
esty and weaken self-respect. The stony-broke
who had seen better days would have died
rather than go to a back door and beg for a
hand-out but he had no scruples against clean-
ing the lunch counter, trying to watch the rye
bread, the Limburger cheese, the bar-keep and
the door leading to the street, all at the same
time.

Gentle methods were not employed in dealing with the drop-ins who moved direct to the
food-trough instead of proceeding to the bar
and giving the house some trade. Many of the
larger places employed special "bouncers"
who watched all who came in and made sure
that only the buyers were having their plates
filled with a menu which would now cost one
dollar at any hotel of the first magnitude.
Both the bouncer and the bar-keep had to ex-

ercise a nice sense of discrimination in sorting out the willing spenders from the dead-beats. They had to be careful and they were. The shabby person who sidled up to the array of eatables and was pronging in all directions and trying to get a couple of square meals for an investment of nothing whatsoever, was out of luck when apprehended.

The Argus-eyed server of drinks could splash out orders to eight customers simultaneously and, at the same time, check up on six free-lunchers and spot a "ringer" with the sureness of a bird-dog flushing a quail. The reason why vagrants so seldom put over their cadging operations was that they looked guilty.

The bar-tender always acted promptly but he was at a great disadvantage. By the time he had secured the bung starter and run all the way to the end of the bar and turned the corner, the hobo had made a flying getaway through the swinging doors and was headed toward the setting sun.

It was the floor-walking bouncer who made life a hell for the boys who were hungry but broke. He had a way of sneaking up from behind. His favorite hold was one hand on the collar and the other taking up the slack in the trousers and when he threw a non-producer for a loss of twenty yards, the victim was out of play. He never came back for more.

Believe it or not, bouncing became a fine art and out of the thousands and thousands of American citizens who were heaved into the street from saloons, dance halls, hotel lobbies and all-night restaurants, it is not on record that the bouncers made one single mistake. In the large and busy eating places which catered to night-hawks of every description the waiters were carefully recruited from the prize-ring stables. Any one of them had tattoo marks on him and could bend a horse-shoe. The staff in the famous nocturnal resort known as "Jack's," just across from the New York Hippodrome, was drilled as carefully as West Point cadets. Those waiters were the friendliest eggs in the world until some one started to rough it up.

Let us pause for a minute to inquire why it is that the sons of the rich, who received early training from tutors and governesses, and then attended the best prep schools and, later, re-

38

BUSINESS MEN'S LUNCH

Gluyas Williams
Courtesy of *Cosmopolitan*

ceived degrees from the more important universities, are usually the ones who want to lick policemen and cabmen, break glassware and forcibly drag chorus girls away from some other table. It is so today and it was just as much so in the halcyon days and nights when "Jack's" was always jammed until broad daylight. The collegians, and others who could not breathe the night air without becoming belligerent, seemed to think that "Jack's" was just the place in which to stage a battle. When fists began to fly and furniture was crashing, the waiters closed in swiftly from all directions. The team-work was wonderful. They gave every disturber of the peace what was known as the "bum's rush." All of the gallant youths who had been fighting to win the approval of blondes or brunettes, or both, found themselves in the middle of Sixth Avenue, looking up at the stars.

Unfortunately for the retail trade, not every saloon could hire a trained bouncer, and the busy bar-keep was handicapped by being compelled to cover a lot of distance, after securing the bung-starter and declaring war. The trade boasted very few Malachy Hogans.

Malachy kept a place on Clark Street, Chicago, half way between the Grand Opera House and the Sherman Hotel. He could vault over the bar and light on an unwelcome caller with all the destructive effect of a horse lying down on a butterfly. He had to inspect the line coming in at the door because his free lunch serving-table was famous for variety and quality. A high-brow editorial writer one day complimented him on his food service.

"That's funny," said Malachy. "Yesterday I was playing pinochle in the back-room with Collector of Port Russell, Archbishop Feehan and Maggie Cline an' they all raved about the lunch, same as you."

Malachy said this to a relative of Martin J. Russell—one of the most dignified, scholarly and well-behaved gentlemen in the city—and the relative walked out, horrified and puzzled.

The raiding of free lunches became almost a steady job and a regular trade for flophouse derelicts and no-goods who were on their uppers, so a great many saloons adopted the rule of giving out food from the bar or handing the customer a ticket which he could take across to the food department and exchange for a bowl of soup.

Here was a sign that you saw behind many a bar:

A fried oyster, a clam or a hard-boiled egg with every drink.

This sounds incredible, but there was a basement place under one corner of the McVicker Theatre Building, Chicago, which specialized on selling beer customers huge wedges of pie at five cents the wedge. You would naturally believe that about a gallon of beer in combination with apple, huckleberry or cocoa-nut pie might form a dangerous explosive. Nevertheless, many of the boys liked pastry with their suds. The show window of that highly-perfumed cellar resort under good old McVicker's always had a vast array of pies arranged in stacks so high that a greyhound couldn't have jumped over them.

Free lunch became an institution because of the well-known zoölogical fact that certain kinds of food promote thirst and any malt fluid with a sharp tang to it encourages hun-

ger. The more lunch the beer-hounds consumed the greater was their enthusiasm for
salty food, and the more pretzels and sardellen
they gobbled up, the more enduring became
the thirst. The net result was a positive dem-
onstration of the fact that the text-book on
physiology, which said that the total capacity
of the human stomach was three pints, was
simply groping in the dark. It was offering
an obsolete theory instead of recognizing plain
facts.

One whole chapter might be devoted to that
vitrified and 8-shaped article of food known
as the pretzel. Because it was so glossy and
offered so much resistance to bad teeth, many
supposed that it belonged to the mineral kingdom. "Biff" Hall, President of the famous
Turn-Over Club, discovered that nearly all
of the pretzels consumed in the middle west
were made at a foundry on the North Side, in
Chicago. He visited the pretzel mill and saw
the whole works in operation. The hand-
carved wooden patterns were imbedded in the
moist sand of the molding-boxes and then
lifted out, leaving hollow spaces into which a
molten fluid could be poured as it came white-

hot from the crucibles. When the pretzels had hardened so that they could be lifted from the sand-boxes they went from the main foundry to another department in which salt was sprinkled on them. Then they went to the cooling room and remained there until they were ready to be carried by overhead cranes to the varnishing-shop. After they had acquired the proper lustre they were ready to be crated and sent to the saloons. Those who clamor for the return of beer say that pretzel foundries cannot be re-opened and run at a profit unless the Volstead Act is modified. The attempt to keep pretzel mills going as noodle factories has not been successful, because the old equipment cannot be utilized. Noodles must be snipped off by hand, after the dough has been worked into an elastic condition, whereas the pretzel has to be cast in hollow molds, the same as automobile parts.

Probably the most valuable of all the thirst-provoking items included in the average free lunch was the limp, silver-coated minnow called the "sardel," a relative of the sardine. Always it was known by the German plural for the name, which was "sardellen." The aristocratic sardine, immersed in olive oil and coming in small cans, was too expensive to be set out in large platters. Furthermore, olive oil counteracts the influence of alcohol. This important discovery was made by the U. S. Navy. But the sardellen, saturated with brine and probably sold by the hogshead, became one of the staple stand-bys of every saloon catering to a reliable beer trade. They were saltier than the Seven Seas and were served whole. No one had tampered with the heads, tails or interior arrangements. They were in great favor because a patron after he had taken a couple of them, draped across a slab of rye bread, had to rush to the bar and drink a lot of beer to get the taste out of his mouth. The sardellen were more than fish. They were silent partners.

As a matter of cold truth, the average free lunch was no feast for Lucullus or "Diamond Jim" Brady, but a stingy set-out of a few edibles which were known to give customers an immediate desire for something to drink. The idea was to set out as much as possible at small expense. Rye bread was always present. Right in the center of the soiled table-cover you might have found a bowl of baked beans and alongside of it a glass of troubled water and in the glass were immersed several forks which, the evidence indicated, had been used in hoisting beans. The thin slices of limber yellow cheese were flanked by a smeary pot of brown mustard with a paddle in it. The common "boloney," which used to sell by the yard instead of the pound, was over-seasoned with pepper, for a definite reason. There might be spring onions and radishes but only when they were plentiful and cheap. Fortunately there was no closed season for dill pickles. In a German place you might find blut-wurst or blood sausage, a dainty made up of coagulated blood which had not been cooked but which had been shot full of salt and black pepper. Or the hard and leathery cervelat or summer sausage. The longer it was kept, the more petrified and tasty it became.

The regulars who went around shopping sometimes discovered pickled pig's feet, but they were more apt to find sauer kraut. If you do not find ripe olives and veal cutlets and imported Gruyere on this list, remember we are describing a saloon and not a "buffet."

Mention must be made of one of the stars of the group, ranking well up with the pretzel and the sardel. Referring, of course, to your old playmate known as the Dried Herring, *alias* the Black-Eyed Susan, *alias* the Blind Robin. He was withered, and shriveled and warped, with dead eyes and tail awry, but the devotees who were fond of former fish that had been imperfectly preserved in salt, preferred him to terrapin. He can still be found at a delicatessen store but his social eminence has departed in spite of the fact that he is first cousin to the patrician kippered herring, known throughout Great Britain as "the drunkard's breakfast."

That's all there is to tell about the typical free lunch. It was just a collection of culls and the main idea was not to provide nourishment but merely excite an undying thirst. The usual free lunch was not calculated to arouse the enthusiasm of an epicure. The spread represented a small investment and would not have been alluring to a teetotaler but the boys nibbled at it between schooners. When a beer-fiend was gulping them down, one after another, he would eat anything except hay.

5

WHAT THEY DRANK

A GOOD bar-tender in a real swagger place during the Pre-War wetness had to acquire almost a liberal education in order to know how to concoct all of the cocktails, rickeys, fizzes, cobblers, punches and other fearful and wonderful compounds. Only an artist of the first rank could properly build up a *pousse café* or permit the absinthe to drip so as to be properly opalescent and sufficiently potent. The hotel mixers had to make punches and "cups," the latter compounded of light wines and mineral water with mint, sliced lemon, pineapple and, very often, long strips of cucumber, floating around like the flotsam in a ferry slip.

Some of the punches made up for private celebrations were about the most deadly output of the sophisticated bar. There was one called Artillery Punch which used cold strong tea as a base and called for portions of brandy, rum and other high-powered distillations.

If you ever saw an unabridged Guide for Bar-Tenders you may recall that it was almost as large as the Family Medicine Book. It contained hundreds of recipes, some of them still known by the names invented in the wild mining and cattle towns of the west and southwest.

In a large bar, catering to a trade which included travelers from everywhere, the lad in the white jacket had to be letter perfect on a repertoire longer than that of a tenor at the Metropolitan. New cocktails were being invented and christened every week. If some genius in New Jersey thought out a combination of apple-jack, plain syrup, diced apples and a dash of lemon juice and called it a "Jack Rose," the artist at the Palace in San Francisco would be all set, within two weeks, to take care of the smartie from the East who strolled in and casually asked for a Jack Rose.

It was a matter of pride with the mixers at the important drinking headquarters to know all about every combination which had come into favor in any part of the country. The supreme humiliation was to be compelled to ask, "How do you make it?" A good Waldorf specialist could put together any one of fifty different cocktails without making a false move or reaching for the wrong bottle. And he would have died of shame if compelled to use a shaker. When plain and fancy bar-room drinking was in flower no one had ever seen in a saloon a silver container with a lid on top and a spout sticking out at the side. The shaker seems to have originated in the British Colonies and it made no headway in the United States until it became a by-product of Prohibition. Probably one explanation is that synthetic stuff has to be chilled to the limit and whipped to a lather, in order to get rid of the liniment taste and make it resemble something to drink.

All mixed drinks were actually mixed, and not scrambled. The high-grade expert, with his heart in his work, went at a julep or a Clover Leaf with all of the care and concentration of one of the Mayos performing a major operation. The ice in the tall glass was crystal clear and the tiny nuggets were of uniform size. Every ingredient was measured. The careless bar-keep, trying to take care of a rush trade, splashed in the gin and the several

Vermouths or fruit juices and insisted that he could get the correct proportions by guesswork, but he was not a true member of the guild.

The supreme art of the mixing process was to place the thumb lightly on top of the long spoon and then revolve the spoon at incredible speed by twiddling the fingers. This was a knack acquired by the maestros only. Thousands of parlor amateurs attempted the twiddle but not one of them ever got it right.

If you were not familiar with what was happening around the bars that have ceased to be, you may now believe that every emporium was the happy hunting grounds for cocktails, cobblers, fizzes and sours. As a matter of cold history, of all the liquid refreshments that were more or less in favor before the hurricane came along, only two staples were in steady demand by the regular trade of the common or garden variety of saloon. These were beer and whisky. Beer for the thirsty and red liquor for those who wished to induce, for at least a brief period, the sense of well-being. To serve drinks in the common run of places required no more technical skill than is needed to put food in

Gluyas Williams

He felt around for the chaser and put out the fire

front of domestic animals. It was just a case of turning the faucet or slamming the old black bottle out on the bar with an empty glass of limited capacity and a "chaser" of plain water—although once in a while a patron with an educated gullet demanded ginger ale, clam juice or even milk.

Regarding the glass into which the slug was decanted, there were certain unwritten rules of etiquette meant to regulate the pouring, but these rules were not always observed. What was known as a "gentleman's drink" never approached the rim. Probably an ounce and a half of dynamite in solution represented the portion which would not cause the clerk to give the buyer a hard look or gently inquire, "Will you need a towel?" The implication was that preparations were under way for the taking of a bath. In the barrel-houses and out-and-out joints it was taken for granted that the glass would be filled to the brim and the receptacle was of stingy capacity but it had to be large enough to contain a real jolt or the trade might be lost to some competitor with a larger heart. Any dealer who served a generous dose for a nickel (and

there were plenty of five-cent places), protected himself by cutting the goods with plain
water and diluted prune juice and sometimes
he added a modicum of red pepper, because
the real toper didn't think he was getting
genuine stuff unless he experienced a scorch-
ing sensation in the palate and along the entire length of the esophagus. Before he could
choke to death he felt around for the chaser
and put out the fire. Not to drink your liquor
straight was considered a sign of effeminacy.
The idea was to uphold a reputation as a he-
man, no matter what happened to the lining of
the stomach.

The drinking habits of the majority during
the decades which preceded the appearance of
Mr. Volstead were entirely different from
those which are now under cover in speak-
easies, soft drink parlors, garages, hay-mows
and the homes of the elite. What are the scofflaws drinking now, if we are to believe all we
read in the magazines? Scotch and gin. Bless
your soul, Scotch was practically unknown in
the common run of saloons of America until
late in the nineties. It seemed to arrive with
golf and spread in popularity as more and

56

more people began to dally with the ancient and honorable pastime. With the sudden demand for many brands of smoky Scotch came the high-ball. No one in the Working Men's Exchange or the Farmers' Home ever heard of such a thing as a high-ball when bar-drinking was prevalent, and if any consumer had insisted on drowning his copper-distilled Kentucky Bourbon in a large quantity of that cheap fluid which they put under bridges or use in sprinkling the lawn, he would have been hooted off the premises. There seemed to be no sense in taking a shot that had been so weakened that it lost the kick and was robbed of all authority.

Just now much of the scandal has to do with gin, if that name can be applied to alcohol secured from grain, sugar or wood, thinned up with distilled water and slightly perfumed with juniper berries or hair tonic. In the olden days gin was not regarded as one of the standbys, except in clubs, hotels and those pretentious cocktail palaces in which the tired business man got himself all primed up to eat twice as much food as he needed. The humble groggery didn't count on much of a turn-over

57

in gin, and when one of the boys ordered it he usually explained, facetiously, that he was taking it for his wife's kidneys. This remark may be cited as a pretty example of the conventional wit which, in saloon conversation, ranked high as a substitute for sane discussion. Also it will serve as a reminder that the trade solemnly believed that gin soothed and alleviated any kind of kidney trouble and that hot "rum and gum" with nutmeg sprinkled on top, was an unfailing cure for a bad cold.

Gin was the dominating theme song of most of the well-known cocktails but your typical dispenser in the saw-dust places didn't want to fuss with cocktails and he had a certain contempt for them as a weak substitute for honest-to goodness liquor and fit only for dudes and weaklings. Tom Moran had a famous place on Randolph Street in Chicago, reputed to carry only the highest grades of pure corn whisky that had been properly aged in wood. His small establishment was regular headquarters for the top aristocracy of Bourbon connoisseurs. Tom drew an occasional mug of beer with extreme reluctance but he absolutely refused to compromise the standing of his establishment by serving any kind of mixed drink. If one of the gentlemen in the line-up expressed a preference for a Gin Daisy or a Dry Martini, Tom simply requested him to leave quietly without causing any disturbance.

Those who railed at the traffic always referred to the retail dealers as "rum sellers" but that was all wrong. They sold very little rum because this dark and highly aromatic distillation was not a drink but merely a guaranteed remedy for bronchitis.

Even if tall drinks were unknown, the seltzer bottle had a place among the bar goods because, very often, the purchaser who began to realize that he was taking on too much cargo compromised on lemon juice and seltzer. It was supposed to "settle the stomach," provided it did not arrive too late. You must know that a large percentage of those who pushed through the swinging doors were not looking for song, persiflage and laughter. They were going in to organize a small clinic and take treatment. Every thirst parlor staged a parade of Early Birds who wanted to get their eyes open and uncoil their nerves and fortify themselves for the dreary hours ahead, knowing that the sun would not come up until the lights had been turned on. Not much conversation during the early day. The barkeep simply threw out the life-line. In the every-day saloon the sunrise bracer was nothing more or less than straight stuff with mighty little water. Some quenched the flames with beer but the tried and true veterans wanted liquor. They didn't have to ask for it. The friend back of the bar was a mind-reader and knew the sign language.

In the onyx-and-gold cafes of the wicked cities the demand was for strange and complicated prescriptions. Chilled absinthe drinks were the most powerful of the pick-me-ups. They lifted the sufferer about a mile in the air and then let him drop into the mud. Shandygaff was a mixture of beer and ginger ale. A combination guaranteed to put dead bodies all over the rugs, and often featured at large parties, was known as "Velvet." It consisted, half and half, of champagne and porter. It drove away the clouds for the time being but had a recoil similar to that of Big Bertha, the German super-gun. A raw egg surrounded by Worcestershire sauce was favored by many who had been in a state of coma and could not bear the sight of food. A mixture of high voltage was known at all of the New York hotel bars as a brain-duster. Every ingredient, including Three-Star Hennessey, was supposed to be good for what ailed the customer. It was an intricate work of art and the bar-keep was supposed to put in everything behind the bar except the Government license.

To drink in the morning was not good form but very often it seemed absolutely necessary to those who had passed through a hard night, with the moon moving from one place to another and the lights of the Aurora Borealis lighting up the heavens not only in the north but also in the west, south and east. Most of those who started out the day by touching the harp gently seemed to agree with the delegate to the state convention who stood at the Denison bar in Indianapolis at 7.30 a.m. and advanced the following opinion: "A drink in the morning will do you no harm unless you let it die later in the day."

61

6

WHY PEOPLE BEHAVE SO

EVEN the most ardent Dry will admit that it is almost impossible to eradicate the daily habits, the social customs and the time-honored practices which have been in evidence and tolerated for centuries—merely by taking a couple of roll-calls in Congress and saying, "Presto, change!"

The saloon had a long start on the anti-salooners. In the excavated city of Pompeii you can go into what is left of the wine-shops and see the massive stone bars and the stone benches for the customers and also mural decorations and carved symbols which prove that these shops were frequented by high-stepping rounders and females who were not all that they should have been. History does not go back far enough to uncover any period during which the wine-bibber could not find a "Welcome" sign in front of some cool retreat within which he could bib as long as his bronze coins held out.

The problem of the Drys has been to uproot traditions—and traditions go a long way back.

The caterers of food and drink were busy during the Rise and Fall of the Roman Empire, the Dark Ages, the Renaissance, the Elizabethan Era, the intellectual reign of Dr. Samuel Johnson and never had business been more rushing than it was in the 19th Century. How many of the elderly men and women of today were brought up on English fiction, with Dickens as the prime favorite? No writer ever put out as much pleasant propaganda in favor of the steaming punch-bowl and the pitcher of cool ale. In every chapter of Dickens some one takes a drink and is patted on the back for it.

How many drinking numbers did you find in The College Song Book? "There is a tavern in the town," "Landlord, fill the flowing bowl," "O, give us a drink, bar-tender," "A stein on the table," "Here's to good old Yale, drink it down," "For tonight we'll merry merry be, and tomorrow we'll get sober," "Down where the Wurzburger flows," "Drink, boys, drink," "Stand to your glasses steady," and one hundred more, not one of which would receive an O.K. from the W. C. T. U. If our most educated citizens put in the best years of their life singing about foaming tankards and ruddy wine, could they be expected to forget the whole hilarious repertoire just because Congress told them to calm down and behave themselves?

Conviviality became imbedded in sentiment, and even people who are short on intellect can be long on sentiment. In all of the Christmas stories and high-life novels of our boyhood there were countless references to tawny Port and rich Burgundy and mulled claret and twinkling champagne, but not one eulogy of malted milk, orange crush or grape juice.

This may seem like a lot of writing about nothing, but you must investigate the ancestry of our present population and consider the influences at work up to a few years ago, in order to understand why so many people who used to be respectable cannot be convinced that it is sinful to serve drinks at a wedding, a christening or a dinner party. They are what they are because they grew on a family tree which produces hard nuts instead of tender blossoms.

64

The sincere Prohibitionist is baffled by the present situation. He never took a drink and never wanted to take a drink and he cannot understand why so many well-to-do families and gay youngsters are flaunting their indifference to certain laws which seem to him to be the very essence of brotherly love and helpful morality. He says that taking a drink is just as illegal and dreadful as taking a narcotic and he can prove it by the statute books. But—did anyone ever read a story of the hero coming back to marry Ethel, of the church bells ringing and villagers cheering, and then the supper in the old oaken hall of the Montagues and Ethel's father, Lord Herbert, standing up to toast the bride and suggesting that everyone present shall arise and take five grains of sulphate of morphia? You never did, any more than you recall a good maritime yarn with the two grizzled sea captains waxing reminiscent over their banana splits.

The fact is that nearly all books of fiction and magazine stories introduced the wineglass, "with beaded bubbles winking at the brim," and surrounded it with adjectives which depicted every bottle of the juice of the grape as a friendly companion rather than a vicious enemy. The reading public was educated to the belief that moderate drinking under polite auspices was an alluring and zestful relief from the monotonies of life, and certainly not sinful. They never had read about a group of jolly good fellows standing around a pump singing "Hail! Hail! The gang's all here!"

I can hear some Dry exclaim: "There you go! You promised to play fair and now you are poking fun at us." Not at all. I am simply trying to bring out and emphasize the fact that all the reading and observation of the scofflaws and their parents and grandparents helped to convince them that an occasional dalliance with certified bottled goods was the most amiable and forgivable of all the small vices; that you had to moisten a dinner party in order to promote conversation, and that a cellar was practically wasted if merely made the home of a furnace which was idle all summer.

Possibly all of the folks who now amaze and infuriate the Drys can be weaned away from their Martinis but the good people who are trying to straighten out the bad ones will never get desired results merely by insisting that

JAMES MONTGOMERY FLAGG..
FROM DEEP MEMORY.

drinking is against the law and therefore it falls into a category with murder, highway robbery and arson. The people who persist in giving cocktail parties don't want to be murderers or bandits or set fire to houses. The reason why they are so hard to handle is that while one of them is rattling the shaker his conscience doesn't hurt him.

What has all this rigmarole to do with the saloon? Just this. Our country is about the only one in which the public house became wholly disreputable. "Saloon," according to the Standard Dictionary, originally meant "a large and elegant apartment for social receptions, for the display of the works of art or for public entertainment." Only in the United States was a common drinking resort known by such a hifaluting title. We started out with taverns and, for a long time, the mugs of ale, the single drams of hard liquor and the filled jugs were passed out at the rear end of every grocery store. Then some enterprising dealer opened a place with mirrors and chandeliers and a picture of Venus Arising from the Bath and the whole lay-out was so elegantine that he decided to call it a "saloon," which is just a variation of salon, than which nothing could be more patrician. It was a high-toned name which very soon began to drag in the mud.

The saloon was responsible for the 18th Amendment and the Volstead Act. For a half century the Prohibition Party held conventions and nominated candidates and adopted platforms without getting anywhere. The towns and counties which went for local option and the state-wide closing up of bars and breweries received no effective help from the Prohibition Party.

In 1892 I reported the National Convention of the Prohibitionists at Cincinnati, sitting on the high platform where I could look out and see the uplifted faces of hundreds of delegates. They were all pop-eyed and seemed to have St. Vitus' dance. The astute Mr. Dickey of Michigan was chairman of the convention and he had some hard-headed plans for organizing and getting votes. He couldn't do anything with the emotional fanatics in front of him. Their idea of saving the world was to sing hymns and pass hysterical resolutions.

But, when the Prohibition Party was

pushed aside, and the grand drive against alcoholic beverages was taken over by The Anti-
Saloon League, things began to happen. If
the organization had called itself The Association against Scotch High-Balls or The Anti-
Cocktail League, it wouldn't have turned a
wheel. Not until the saloon was singled out
and called by name and attacked with heavy
artillery by non-partisan influences, did the
godly millionaires shout "Hurrah!" and begin
to send in those fat checks which enabled
Wayne B. Wheeler to mobilize his vast army
of women, church members, staid farmers and
prim school-teachers. He was given a club with
which to threaten Senators, Congressmen and
state legislators and it is a matter of open
history that most of them began to tremble
and take orders.

If the drinking, previous to 1920, had been
confined to clubs, restaurants and private living quarters, is it probable that there would
have been any wide-spread indignation which
readily crystallized into a concerted and busi-
ness-like attack on all beverages supposed to
contain a dangerous percentage of the old
trouble-maker?

If the League made an error of judgment it was in assuming that the saloon was a synonym for the drink habit. When it came to the grand show-down and the battle against distilleries, breweries and all the wholesale and retail dealers resulted in a sudden whang-bang victory, even the steady patrons, accustomed to resting one foot on the rail, could not come into the open and advance any plausible defense for the saloon.

The millions of good people who asked for the important Amendment and the sweeping provisions of the Volstead Act sincerely believed that the closing up of saloons would result in the depopulation of state prisons and jails, fewer matriculations at the insane asylums, the purification of youth and a new-found happiness in every home. Perhaps they overlooked the fact that Human Nature is closely related to the mule and the most popular horticultural product, since the curtain went up in the Garden of Eden, has been the Forbidden Fruit. All of which is not by way of suggesting that the experiment has been a failure and that some of us are wholly wrong and others are wholly right.

We are talking about the old-time saloon and insisting that it was the culprit responsible for present conditions. It is supposed to be in the past tense but it still blocks the legalizing of light wines and beer. The Canadian provinces tried Prohibition and then went back to Wetness, but not to bar-rooms. In Canada, in Great Britain and in nearly every country in the world, except the United States, the resident or the transient can get it without going out at night, wearing a mask and rubber boots. Did you ever stop to think that this fierce and unrelenting opposition to the manufacture or sale of any fluid with a kick in it is largely due to the fact the saloon is still held in abhorrence because it made a joke of just and reasonable laws? In all other important nations the licensed dealer closed when he was told to close, humbly took orders from the police department and had a wholesome fear of the courts. Here at home the typical saloon-keeper pooh-poohed the statutes, subsidized the police and never figured that he was in danger of a conviction unless he committed a murder in the presence of many witnesses. Not all of the retailers went outlaw but the percentage of

73

those who defied the regulations and outraged the decencies of life was simply appalling. It was the brazen and brutal old-time saloon that bred the furious prejudice against things to drink.

LOW COST OF
HIGH-ROLLING

BECAUSE prices demanded by boot-leggers and speak-easies are so extortionate that they become almost prohibitive to one "who is on pleasure bent but has a frugal mind," a vast amount of misinformation concerning drink-stuffs is afloat among younger people and the older ones who never made an intensive study of the two staples—hard liquor and frothing beer. There was a period, not so remote, when the most powerful stimulants were cheaper than the soda water concoctions of today, by capacity measure.

A few years ago an old building at West Point, Indiana, was torn down. It had stood on a hill overlooking the placid Wabash and below it, almost one hundred years ago, there had been a steam-boat landing. The venerable clapboard structure had been a tavern when it was young. It supplied hard drink to the rivermen and to the farmers for miles around.

Between the walls of the building, as it was being wrecked, were found several sheets of paper which must have slipped through a crack, probably from a shelf back of the bar. They were well preserved pages of a day-book and revealed the prices paid for stimulants along about 1835. The standard price for jug whisky was twenty-five cents per gallon and the average customer seemed to use up about a gallon a week, or a grand total of one dollar for one whole month of mellow indifference to weather conditions, politics, religion and foreign trade. And now it costs a dollar to get an oblong dish paved with little olives.

The standard prices from the time of the Civil War up into the gay nineties were: five cents for beer and ten cents for a pour-it-yourself portion of hard stuff or the common run of mixed drinks, such as cocktails, toddies or fizzes. California remembered the fancy prices of the gold rush days and held out for at least a "bit" as a fair charge for a dram of red essence. "Bit" means twelve and one-half cents. "The long bit" was fifteen cents and the "short bit" was a dime. When the city bars first whooped prices, under high-license pressure, the rule was to serve two whiskies for two bits. The customer who planked down a quarter, and then gave a solo performance of nearly choking to death, received one helping of straight goods and a brass check which could be exchanged for another dose of the same remedy. A wave of indignation swept our fair land when the price went sailing up from a dime to a "bit." There was more protesting when the brass checks went out of circulation and any beverage of high alcoholic content brought fifteen cents in the marts of trade. That fifteen-cent rate, now conceded to be a bargain price, continued in the swell and showy places almost up to the grand shutdown at the time of the World War. And don't forget that during this generous era the wine-cards in good hotels and restaurants were offering the standard (not vintage) champagnes, such as Mumm, or Moet and Chandon, or Cliquot, at $1.75 the pint or $3.50 the quart. Any one who owned up to paying five a bottle for "giggle soup" just the same as confessed that he had done his buying at some establishment not supposed to be mentioned in polite

77

society. Drinks became expensive because of the revenue tax, plus the government license, plus the local license, plus the high rentals, plus the enforced contributions to political campaigns, plus the free lunch and general overhead, and buying tickets for balls and bazaars. The boot-legger escapes these intermediate levies. No wonder that he wears silk shirts!

While we are on the subject of beverages made from grain, it may surprise you to know that powerful intoxicants were being made at very low production cost right up to the time when the important Amendment popped up like a ghost in the middle of the road on a dark night. While out in the southern end of California, working on the outline of a movie, it was my privilege to motor a good deal with a pleasant gentleman who had retired after manufacturing more whisky than ever had been made by any one man in the history of the world. He didn't show any signs of remorse but he was bursting with inside information regarding the mighty industries which he had managed along the river front in Peoria. For instance, he said that one bushel of corn, properly dealt with, would make three gallons of whisky good enough for any one who wanted that kind of a drink. In the early nineties, when corn went as low as fourteen cents a bushel at the rural elevators of Illinois, Indiana and Iowa, the distilleries were turning out whisky which cost them less than ten cents a gallon, counting overhead, depreciation, insurance and everything. He said they could always figure the production cost within a fraction of a cent.

When corn is distilled it comes out of the condenser as a pale and transparent fluid, similar to the native "shine" of the southern hills. That amber color, so greatly admired by the good judges, results from treatment and putting the stuff away in charred barrels for a period of years.

The most amazing information coming from the expert was that the so-called aging of whisky was more or less bunk and founded upon foolish traditions. He said that new liquor that had been properly put through the still was no more harmful as a beverage than the spirits which had been kept in a barrel in a cellar for twenty years. The five-cent slugs handed out in the slum dives and the barrel-houses were not any more dangerous than the rare old nectar served in the homes of the rich and the fastidious clubs. The only trouble was that the cheap places sometimes adulterated the product. He said, furthermore, that in each distillery there had been a keg of this "high wine" or freshly-made pale whisky put right out where all employees could get it, with a few tin-cups around. He said they drank it out of tin-cups for years and most of them lived to be eighty years old. This is not propaganda. I am simply telling you what he told me.

He was not the only one to believe that strong drink seldom bit like a serpent or stung like an adder. Long before Prohibition came along and complicated matters, we had from Indiana in Washington an eminent statesman who was rather strait-laced at home but who, it seems, was not offended when some one in Washington suggested that a slight libation might be poured upon the altar of friendship. One day while Congress was in session a prominent divine who lived in the same town with the eminent statesman, went into the Sen-

EASY ON THE PINCH BOTTLE BOYS-

ate Chamber in search of the distinguished
law-maker but he couldn't find him so he wandered over to the restaurant, which at that
time had all of the trimmings of a night club,
except music and a girl seated on a piano.
The Presiding Elder walked in on the Senator
just as the Senator was pouring what is tech-
nically known as a "hooker" of corn liquor and
he wasn't pouring any dose intended for a
child. The preacher was horrified.

"Oh, Senator!" he exclaimed. "In all the
years I have known you I never suspected that
you were addicted to the use of rum."

"This is not rum," replied the Senator, "this
is copper-distilled Bourbon."

"There is no difference."

"My friends from Kentucky, who ought to
know, say there is all the difference in the
world."

"Whisky is the curse of these United States.
I am surprised to think——"

"Listen, you don't understand, I am doing
this on the advice of my physician. Investi-
gators have recently discovered that the Potomac River, from which we must draw our
water supply, is swarming with deadly germs

—millions and millions of them. Fortunately they have also discovered that if you will mix this Potomac water with high-proof Kentucky liquor, about half and half, the germs expire in the most horrible agony."

While playing golf at French Lick, I had several long talks with a man who had made enough gin to float the American Navy. He supplied it by the barrel to hotels, clubs and private bars, to wholesale dealers, such important food-and-drink shops as Park & Tilford, in New York and Jevne's in Chicago. He told me something new and it may be new to you, even if it is ancient history. He said that gin was obtained by taking the high-wine as it comes from the distillery and putting it through again, permitting the vapors from the vat to pass through a drum in which are many perforated shelves or pans. In these pans are placed juniper berries, acacia buds, lemon peel, orange peel and various assortments of aromatic berries and roots and fruit rinds. The vapors absorb these flavors and when they are condensed in the "worm" they come out at the tail end as a sparkling beverage with an aroma or "bouquet" which, he said, the private citizen who makes it in the kitchen in five minutes can never obtain. He made very harsh comments on some of the home-made imitations of his former brand of goods.

The department stores sold a lot of powerful bottled goods previous to the World War. What was supposed to be excellent gin sold at the cut price of 75 or 80 cents a bottle. One window would be filled with Green River, Clark's, Old Crow, Hermitage, Old Tub, Monongahela and a dozen other kinds of high-proof liquor and the uniform price was one dollar for the full-size bottle and a cut in the price if the buyer took a case. Even champagne of the recognized brands might be obtained for a little over $2 a quart by the case. French wines, Rhine wines, Italian Chianti and all the known kinds of "liqueurs" were incredibly cheap. Between the producer of the grain and grapes were three or four middleman profits, to say nothing of the cost of transportation, storage and bottling. The actual cost of making the stuff wasn't so much. It was the revenue tax, in combination with local high license, which compelled or induced the retailer to charge fifteen cents for two cents' worth of whisky and five cents for one cent's worth of high-collared beer served in a "scuttle." The can customers who "rushed the growler" and came in to get their malt product in pitchers and buckets, expected to get and did get about four liberal helpings for a dime. Figure in the free lunch expense and the overhead for protection and you will begin to understand why so much beer served in the dingy and bargain-counter places was made of cheap materials, delivered while "green" and that it held only small percentages of genuine hops and malt.

Now, if you want to stagger in the imagination, consider the following facts: A bushel of corn can be converted into three gallons of whisky, much less dangerous than the synthetic "alky" being distributed by the illicit dealers. At the present writing, corn is being delivered at the country elevators for thirty-six cents a bushel. Making the most generous estimate for the expense of building the fire and cooking the mash and drawing off the moonshine, the cost of whisky to any one familiar with the routine of distillation is about twenty cents a gallon. There are eight gills to the quart or thirty-two to the gallon. The former bar-tender figured that a quart of the red stuff was good for twenty drinks, and if a few gentlemen dropped in, the number might be raised to twenty-five. Let us make allowance for the fact that possibly larger drinks are now being taken, say fifteen to the quart. The speak-easy sells for $15 something which actually cost about five cents and the total profits going to somebody for a $10 bottle of spurious Scotch or compounded rye delivered to a hotel bed-room run to about 20,000 per cent. The stingy bottle of beer can be manufactured, bottled, capped and crated for a grand total of two cents. When it retails at fifty cents the intermediate profits may be roughly estimated at 2400 per cent.

The production plants operate in smaller units and probably, their incidental expenses have increased, but, just the same, you can't take all the lead pencils in the world and figure out anything except the most amazing and ridiculous profits for all who handle outlaw beverages. Something to think about. Not wet —not dry—just history.

8

THE BAR-KEEP

UP to the present time this story of the old-time saloon has been somewhat punctuated by abuse. In a desire to be unbiased, the author has gone out of his way to tell many unpleasant facts about what the old ladies with the silver specs used to call "hell-holes." But there are two sides to every story and every cloud has some kind of a lining and Mr. Emerson was right when he expounded the Law of Compensation and insisted that good people who seemed to be fortunate had some evil traits and several woes concealed in their private egos and those members of society who seemed lost to all the conventions of morality might blossom into calla lilies under encouraging conditions.

Most certainly we will not be giving a correct picture of the licensed liquor shop merely by insisting that the resort itself and the operating staff and the purchasers were utterly disreputable. The Saloon Business went on the rocks because the proprietors of the drinking places and their business associates and supporting patrons were committed to an elastic code governing methods of management, political expedients, private conduct and the assertion of human rights which did not jibe and fit in with the modern drive for industrial efficiency or with that consuming craze for purification and reform which raged from 1917 to 1920, often raising the temperature of an ardent church-worker to above 102.

The saloon, as an institution, was doomed from the moment it appeared in the dock and pleaded "Not Guilty" and went on trial for high crimes and misdemeanors. The character witnesses who dared to show up were quite a help to the prosecution. The jury was packed with women and deacons and members of the choir. The verdict went the limit and was applauded at the time. If the booze-seller and the bar-tender escaped the electric chair it was only because those who pronounced sentence could not find anything in the books which authorized a death penalty. The boys had been sowing the wind and they reaped a Florida hurricane which uprooted every saloon and

89

carried it away, leaving nothing behind to mark the site except a lingering aroma.

Because the retailing of drink was attacked with so much ferocity during those emotional years of the World War and hysterical home-comings and high-tension readjustments, the rabid anti-salooners have hardly had time to cool out and get back to normalcy. Even now they growl inwardly and begin to froth a little at the mouth when the word "saloon" is mentioned. They still insist that any one who is not Prohibition has to be pro-saloon. Defending the saloon is just as impossible as defending Benedict Arnold, John Wilkes Booth, Guiteau, or Mr. Luetgert, of Chicago, who became annoyed one morning, because his wife served cold coffee, and so he ran her through a sausage-machine.

But it may not be extreme treason or distortion of history to say that some of the dealers possessed human qualities which distinguished them from the brute creation and many a bar-keep had a sympathetic heart beating beneath his white, or once-white, jacket and his attitude toward the problems of life was benign rather than cruel. He was a just

MOPPING UP

R. L. Goldberg

arbiter when disputes arose, and how they did arise! A patient listener to long and rambling narratives. A fair-minded referee when it came to deciding wagers concerning the dates and details of major sporting events. Always a peace-maker and never a promoter of assault and battery.

He had to deal with assorted humanity and attune himself to all of the moods which over-came consumers who went out of gear after the third round had been served. Drink had a way of transforming the timid shoe salesman into a noisy debater and bringing to him the delusion that he could overcome, in physical combat, either a brakeman or a blacksmith. It caused large muscular men who, in working hours, were either surly or reticent, to weep softly or burst into song. It brought on earn-est discussions which had to do with political issues or social problems. It encouraged the lowly to assume airs of grandeur and it urged the under-dog to advertise his importance and relate his inmost grievances to any one who would listen, and, usually, the bar-keep had to do the listening.

It may be a surprise to many readers to

learn that the experienced bar-keep had a sorry opinion of drinkers in general. Privately, and not for publication, he could deliver a temperance lecture which would have done credit to Father Mathew, John B. Gough or William Jennings Bryan. Furthermore, he had more first-hand information regarding the effects of drink than could be acquired by any platform evangelist.

If he was a first-class bar-tender and true to the creed of his exacting profession, he was a total abstainer or drank in extreme moderation outside of business hours. His first rule of conduct was not to do any nipping while "on watch." If you are old enough you may remember the popular song which started off as follows:

> "I never drink behind the bar,
> But I will take a mild cigar."

At this point we might digress and work in one whole chapter regarding the saloon cigar. It was light in color and loosely wrapped and came out of a box decorated with gold and bright colors but there was a general belief that it was made from lettuce instead of tobacco. A real Corona would have been wasted on any sincere drinker who was working at his trade. A diplomatic bar-keep collected these ultra-Colorados all day and, at closing-time, put them back into the box and took credit on the cash register. Of course, if strongly urged by some belligerent, he might compromise by taking a "snit" of beer. The snit was a private glass, kept on the work-table underneath the bar. It was about the size of an eye-cup and the supposed drink was all foam. The dispenser could take a hundred "snits" without knowing that he had received a message.

In any place with the slightest pretense to class, the bar-keep wore approved regalia. The white and starched coat had on the lapel a geranium with a small fern as a background and silver foil around the stem. Always the linen was spotless, the white four-in-hand carried a sparkling solitaire, sometimes tinged with yellow but always lustrous. He was cleanly shaven, favored the moustache as an adornment, and the well-oiled hair described a festoon across the forehead. Certainly a picture, with the wide mirror and the dazzling crystal as a background.

If he worked in one of the sardellen places,

it was a safe bet to call him "Otto." If undeniably Irish, there was no chance of offending him by calling him "Mike." If the refectory happened to be in a small town and the servitor needed a shave and was minus the immaculate costume and had blue elastics around his biceps, it was perfectly proper to hail him as "Bill."

Reference has been made to the bar-keep as a diplomat. Once in so often, if a group of enthusiastic buyers had been pushing important money across the moist mahogany, he was expected to announce, smilingly and suavely, "Gents, this one is on the house," thereby establishing himself as one of nature's noblemen.

The tradition is that he and every other purveyor of distilled and malt liquors enticed men to drink and plied them with all sorts of devastating beverages and were brutally indifferent to the welfare of the regulars. Well, there were all kinds of saloons, just as there are now all kinds of barber shops. The keeper of the barrel-house was usually a gorilla but at least a majority of the ordinary drinking places didn't like to keep on serving a customer who was obviously far gone and becoming either maudlin or disorderly. Goodness knows, the retail traffic had enough to answer for, and it is plain slander to say that all of them wanted to serve to drunks and minors and have back rooms for the wild girls and take a rake-off on poker games and operate with trained dice and tolerate all the rowdies of the neighborhood. It was not until the saloons multiplied until each one had to resort to "rough stuff" in order to get money into the till that the urbane proprietor who wished to run a "nice, quiet place," and his humane helper, with genuine scruples against peddling to boys or building up a case of delirium tremens, became lost in the shuffle.

You have not been accurately informed regarding the old-time saloon if you have been led to believe that all bar-keeps were low and bestial characters. They were profitably employed in a business which was sanctioned by law and approved by custom and encouraged by the patronage of doctors, lawyers, merchants, farmers, mechanics and all the other influential citizens within drinking distance of the bar, except a disregarded minority which preferred prayer-meetings to convivial drinking parties. The saloons did one hundred times as much business as the prayer-meetings and the genial bar-keep was more of a public character and more highly esteemed by the crowd than the pale and pious preacher. The latter attacked the saloon from the pulpit but the saloon did not even know it was being attacked.

The aura of loving regard which surrounds the memory of the favorite bar-keep of every veteran Wet is a somewhat damp fog, and the dampness may be distinctly traced to a volatile fluid distilled from the grains of the field, but it is a genuine regard. The authentic bar-keep is a thing of the past. He was sentenced to soft-drink parlors or banished into oblivion. He was at least as human and humane as his contemporaries and much more temperate in his habits. Let his epitaph be kindly.

THE REGULARS

IN the decades preceding the ones which we are now trying to live through, it is well to remember that the restless American public had to get along without movies or talkies, radio entertainments in the front room, low-priced motor cars in which to go gadding about on cheap gasoline, free public libraries, or any other recreations except theatrical shows and baseball games in the cities, riding the bicycle, both in the cities and the small towns, and, not to be overlooked, wandering toward the headquarters for hilarity where the lights were bright and joy was unrefined and drinks were cheap.

Not one-half of one per cent of the male population belonged to clubs. The church could not compete with the saloon as a social center because it was about as cheerful as a mausoleum while the place on the corner reeked with the kind of unrestrained gayety which has been in partnership with original sin since the beginning of history. What's more, the church was open about four hours every week and the saloon was open at least 108 hours and the city places were open 7 times 24, or 168 hours. Most of the churches harbored small groups of sedate men and women who were already saved and sanctified and ticketed for future rewards. The saloon gave boisterous welcome to every male adult, regardless of his private conduct, his clothes, his manners, his previous record or his ultimate destination. The saloon was the rooster-crow of the spirit of democracy. It may have been the home of sodden indulgence and a training school for criminality, but it had a lot of enthusiastic comrades. Bishop Potter was right when he said it was "the poor man's club," and he might have added that the poor man dropped in every night to pay his dues.

The number of men who did not find home any too attractive, or who were in wrong at their own firesides, and who, therefore, were wont to wander out into the night air, simply couldn't think of any good place to go except one of those places. In the old days pool and billiards were not played except at the White

100

Front and the Gem. Besides, the harness-shop closed soon after sundown—and had nothing on tap while it was open and smelled too much of leather. There were plenty of excuses.

The average workaday mortal craved, in the evening, a hearty recognition of his merits as a man, lively intercourse with persons of his own social rating, bantering conversation, laughter and song. The saloons naturally attracted a lot of regulars. Therefore the saloons died of over-popularity.

Because the keeping of a saloon seemed an easy way of making a living, while surrounded by jovial acquaintances, a great number of citizens, who were too lazy or too fat to lay bricks or nail on shingles, applied for licenses. What happened to the saloons is now happening to the filling-stations. If we had one-third as many filling-stations as now border the main highways, all of them would be making money. And, if the United States could have struggled along with about one-fourth as many saloons as it had to tolerate during the thirty years previous to 1920, Prohibition might have been postponed or averted.

Any one of us can sit down now and write

a volume on the Horrors of Overproduction. We have too much wheat, so the farmers are being pauperized and the unemployed of the cities are standing in line and begging for bread, while thousands upon thousands of poor Chinese are starving to death. We have too much wool, therefore no one can get a new suit of clothes. We have a vast oversupply of building material, so the unfortunates are without shelter and must sleep in the parks.

In the eighties and nineties saloons became so plentiful that they were an offense to every street scene and blotches on every landscape. So the wiping-out process began with local option and moved on to state-wide Prohibition, and had its grand climacteric in the 18th Amendment and the Volstead Act. The regulars were without homes, but all the legislation had not altered their instincts or abated the daily thirst.

This history, to be true, must again and again revert to an overwhelming Fact which probably represents the true inwardness of the present perplexities regarding the enforcement of Prohibition. All during the long campaign against the retail traffic, the Bone Drys

took it for granted that all those who offered
no resistance to the closing of the saloons were
publicly and privately against the use of any
kind of alcoholic beverages. This has been the
champion delusion of the present century.
You can and I can list a hundred men and
women who have always been regarded as
moral uplifters, who have certain church con-
nections and send their youngsters to Sunday
School and who are full of civic pride and conventional scruples, and every one of them will,
when the settings are proper and the tempter
uses polite language, absorb home brew or the
Canadian import, take on a few cocktails or
dally with high-balls which are guaranteed not
to destroy the eye-sight. They represent the
new crop of "regulars." Any one who disputes
this statement must be asleep all afternoon and
all evening, with the blinds pulled down. Not
wet—not dry—just history.

However, we started out to talk about the
regulars of the wide-open days and to show
why their steadfast loyalty to the bar-rooms
was responsible for the general prejudice
against the old-time saloon.

The writer started out with a stern resolve

103

not to be guilty of statistics, but the present ignorant generation should be given a few startling figures. A while back I referred to the boyhood home town and the four saloons. These four emporiums, down by the railway station, drew their entire trade from a total population of about 1600, counting all the farmers within a few miles. There were sixteen other drinking places within a radius of fifteen miles, so this writing is not fancy fiction. Of the 1600 persons within our own little zone at least 1200 were women or children below voting age. That left 400 men who had to support the four grog-shops. Many of them were blue-ribboners and church members, actively opposed to any kind of tippling. The partakers may have been in the majority, but of the 400 most certainly there were at least 160 who never spent a red cent in any saloon. That left 240 consumers. It is simple arithmetic. No saloon could count on more than about 60 dependable patrons. Many of these were moderate drinkers of beer. The others had to spend freely to keep four saloons going, and they *did* keep going.

Mention was made of the college town with

20,000 population and 94 saloons. One saloon for every 212 residents. In the near-by villages were more saloons. No kind of figuring can alter the fact that the average bar had a grand total of only about fifty supporters. The same ratio held true in all parts of the corn belt before local option began to drive the drink shops into the centers of population. Is it any wonder that the booze-merchant, after paying for his government license and local license, and making campaign contributions and paying his rent and holding up his credit with wholesalers and brewers, had to hustle to get any profits?

He did the only thing he could do, and that was to encourage the spending proclivities of his own little group of bar-flies. The "regulars" were roughly divided into two groups— one consisting of those who dropped in and drank and departed, the other made up of the ever-thirsty, who kept hanging around and waiting for some one to come in and order all present to "belly up to the bar," and the evening roysterers who were violently opposed to going home early.

Always the old-time saloon had at least a

couple of derelict hangers-on who showed up early, to sweep out and empty the fly-traps and crack the ice and set the stage for another performance. They received no money but got the compensation they wanted—about two raps of the hard stuff and the remnants of free lunch. They stayed around to do menial chores and sponge enough pick-ups to keep them alive and semi-conscious for another day.

Reference has been made to the morning drinkers who came one at a time and partook without delay or ceremony. Among them might have been found the dignified lawyer who could not plead a criminal case until he had fortified himself with a special brand of high-proof goods. Also the veteran of the Civil War who had to kill a lingering pain in the region of the wound received at Chickamauga. Also the printer who had to fix himself so that he could see which type to pick up. And many others to whom the early dram was not by way of celebration but merely a necessity of life.

Beer-lovers kept dropping in all day. Farmers helped the afternoon trade. They paid cash for their Old Crow and what they bought at the general store went on the charge account.

Except on Saturdays the daylight buying was inclined to drag a little but all the stars came out soon after nightfall. That was when the genuine regulars arrived early and stayed late and demonstrated, over and over again, that they could drink it or leave it alone. Sometimes the getting-together was a love-feast and at other times it was a Donnybrook. Whether a jubilee or a massacre, it was help-ing to give the saloon a bad name. All of those wives waiting at home were not thinking pleas-ant thoughts about the place on the corner. No one supposed that they would ever find it possible to get back at Mr. Saloon-Keeper. Hardly any one supposed that anything could happen to put him into the side-pocket. Hardly any one even dreamed of what was going to come off in 1920. Some of them do not believe it, even now.

10

SENTIMENT—TRADITIONS

IT harbored a bleary crew. It was smelly. It made no deliberate effort to improve the niceties of conduct or elevate the tone of conversation. The old-time saloon was a rowdy and always under suspicion, because wearing a mask. In any sober council of the representative business institutions of a community, it was just as welcome as an illegitimate son at a family reunion. It was coddled around election time but feared and not highly respected during the long intervals between political campaigns.

To the ladies of the W. C. T. U. and the black alpaca ministry and the milk-drinking teetotalers it was just the unspeakable lair of heartless villains who dragged the poor workingman in from the street, used cunning methods to induce him to partake of fiery poisons, and then sent him home to beat his wife. The keeper was always Simon Slade, the hardened rum-seller of "Ten Nights in a Bar-Room," and every one who quaffed at the bar was Joe Morgan, the village sot.

In making a fair appraisal of the old-time saloon and sizing it up in perspective, there can be no denial of the fact that it was the bad boy of the neighborhood, but the boy had certain human and generous qualities. The enemies discovered only the most revolting traits and painted all their pictures in dark colors.

The truth was somewhere in between the slanderous implications of the church element and the affectionate tributes paid by those who regarded the bar-room as a delightful haven for those who were harried and world-ridden.

Bless your soul, the drink-parlor was a very hot-bed of sentiment. It was a hatchery for romantic inspiration and a factory which turned out enormous quantities of brotherly love. True, the sentiment usually bordered on that kind of sentimentality known as "mush." The aroused spirit of romance never led on to heroic deeds but merely to heroic conversation. The feeling of brotherly love was bona fide, but it was often known to evaporate later on when the gauge indicated that the pressure was steadily falling and the fraternal jubilee was about to be followed by a mild case of bust-head.

Men left their families to loiter in saloons, but this did not mean that they ceased to love their families. It was right in front of the bar that the fond husband announced to the wide world that his wife was the best damned house-keeper in town and her kitchen floor was so clean that you could eat off of it. And, as Charley Case once remarked, they often did. The birth of another infant, the graduation of Myrtle from the high school or the junior getting a grade of 100 in geography, called for the immediate purchase of a round of drinks.

Some of the proprietors and their first lieu-tenants were most observant and had a ready wit. Their comments on men and affairs were often to the point and worth repeating. Men-tion has been made of Malachy Hogan, than whom a more captivating red-head never drew the breath of life. When Maurice Barrymore and Wilton Lackaye were playing in Chicago they spent countless hours with Malachy, be-cause he was an endless delight. Then there was "Jim" McGarry, who kept a place in

Dearborn Street. His hard-boiled philosophy and caustic sarcasm provided the first inspiration for the inimitable "Dooley" pieces by "Pete" Dunne. When George Silver graduated as bar-keep for "Bath-House John" Coughlin and opened a place of his own, George Cohan was the first customer and paid a thousand dollars for a pint of champagne, just to prove that he had enjoyed hearing Mr. Silver call things by their right names. Not forgetting "Hinky-Dink," who kept a Clark Street place that ran from street-front to alley and swarmed with the down-and-outers. He was an intelligent, suave, diplomatic and highly entertaining little monarch, even if he was a wholesale dealer in floating voters. All of which is by way of suggesting that saloons were not given over entirely to dull low-brows.

Here is what you might have heard in any small town:

"Doc Cleghorn would have the biggest practice in town if he'd leave liquor alone."

"Dan Silsby knows more law than all the rest of 'em put together an' is just naturally brighter'n a whip, but he drinks too much."

"It's too bad about Henry. He's the only

111

dentist within fifty miles that knows how to make an upper plate but he's always so full of forty-rod he don't know an upper from a lower."

And so on. It was the fashion for orators and scholars and grizzled heroes of 1861 to 1865 to imbibe more or less, with chances favoring the "more." Consequently, eloquence and learning and patriotism were often erupting in the saloons, whereas they should have been saved for important occasions. To deny this, is to confess total ignorance of conditions in towns and small cities during the eighties and nineties.

Yes, indeed! The saloon was the fountainhead of sentiment, which gushed as freely as the beer and contained about the same percent of vitamins.

Traditions were honored and holidays observed. When a comrade departed, eulogies were pronounced and grief was becomingly drowned. The looming figures of American history were held in reverence and the mantle of charity was draped over many a public hero who was known to have his little shortcomings. The Salvation lassie could jingle her tambourine in the lowest dive without fear of annoyance or insult. Theoretically, the drinking classes approved of all plans for bettering the world if these plans did not involve sumptuary legislation. They believed in the Rights of Man, the sanctity of womanhood, the dignity of organized labor, the Declaration of Independence and Santa Claus. When the wind was from the right quarter and all sails were taut, they even forgave their enemies. What a mistake to assume that all of the recent Rip van Winkles were abandoned wretches! They were good to everybody except themselves and those dependent upon them for support.

Every holiday and feast-day in the calendar was remembered and celebrated. Not by closing up, in strict observance of certain unreasonable laws, but by giving the emotional patrons a chance to assemble, either openly or by way of the convenient rear entrance, and discuss the importance of the anniversary.

St. Patrick's Day was one of the high spots for every place in which the lad in the jacket was known as "Mike" instead of "Otto." If you are on the lucky side of forty, possibly you never heard of the Irish Question. For a good many years we heard plenty. The Question was answered every night in many a saloon. If three sons of the sod got together, the business before the house was to recite "Shamus O'Brien" and free Ireland. Queen Victoria was a good woman, but no one ever saw her picture alongside that of John L. Sullivan. The organized bitterness against England is just as quiescent now as free silver, but it raged for a long time, and a couple of drinks never calmed down any good Fenian who wanted to attack the British Lion.

It was Tom Heath, of McIntyre and Heath, who was chased out of the Irish place on St. Patrick's Day because he ate the shamrocks on the bar, thinking they were watercress. He always insisted that they were very good, with mustard. He might have got into worse trouble if he had ordered an orangeade.

At Christmas and New Year's the old-time saloon attained the heights of popularity, because the management wrote holiday greetings on the mirror, by the use of soap, decorated the dump with wreaths and provided free "Tom and Jerry" for all regulars. A huge bowl was in stage center. It contained a compound which looked like rich custard and acted like chain lightning. The mixture of cream and sugar and beaten eggs was made important by the addition of rum or brandy or whisky or all three. A shaving mug was filled half way up with the gooey confection, after which hot water was added and the foamy surface was flecked with nutmeg, after which came peace on earth and good will toward men.

Rum was usually the foundation of every holiday hand-out, including the popular eggnog. Apple-jack could perfume the breath, but it was mild and innocuous compared with Medford Rum. Any one who drank eight mugs of Tom and Jerry could arise next morning and see his breath. It was something like a search-light, only reddish in tinge. A man in Terre Haute once put in all of New Year's Day absorbing egg-nogs and whatever is the plural of Tom and Jerry. On the morning of January 2nd, in proceeding from his residence to his office, he had to turn a corner on which there was a large retail meat-market. In front of this butcher-shop were some sharp hooks on which to hang the quarters and halves of carcasses. The man made too short a turn and his breath caught on one of the hooks.

Probably a compiled short-hand report of all the talk ever spilled in all the saloons would not make educational reading and could never get past the censor, but be assured that many of the inspiring emotions were genuine, even if somewhat curdled, and the kind-hearted citizen who took off from the drab dullness of his every-day routine and went riding in the ether looked down at the world from benevolent heights and felt altruistic resolves surging within him, but he couldn't remember all of them next day.

It is not contended that the old-time saloon was exactly the same as a florist's shop, but it did maintain an atmosphere of good cheer along with the other atmosphere that you could cut with a knife. There was much hand-shaking and boisterous welcoming and friendship, of a certain kind, flourished like the green bay tree. Gambrinus, in overalls and a flannel shirt, always received a free schooner when he rolled in the kegs and was wished many happy returns of the day. Those who had been wounded in the battle against circumstances

116

could find soothing words and first-aid treatment. Traditions and customs were based upon the broad-minded assumption that one man was just as good as another, and possibly better. The more sentimental the talk, the more sympathetic the listening. Rainbows could be seen, even when the sky was overcast. Hope sprang eternal and future prospects were seldom dismal. The prevailing happiness may have been synthetic but it was a pleasant asset while it lasted. To the regulars the saloon was a pal and not an enemy. Of course they were seeing mirages through the alcoholic mists, but they enjoyed the scenery before it was taken away from them.

11

SONG AND STORY

AS a further proof that the old-time saloon
was the home of sentimental traditions and
popular verse and harmonized choral effects, it
is evident to any one that the humble citizen
who has the urge to recite poetry or listen to
folk-songs or be a rough second tenor in a
close-harmony quartet that is tearing the lining out of "Way down yonder in the corn-
field," now has absolutely no place to which
he can go and blow off his stored-up emotions.
Those who officiated at the carrying out of the
death sentence against the liquor shops always
insisted that the average workman or small-
salaried minion who could not find an open
bar-room would soon have more money in the
savings bank and be enabled to pay the rent
and provide the wife and children with clothes
and shoes and show up on Monday morning
without any cob-webs in the cranium and be a
more efficient unit in the complicated machinery of production and distribution. The Anti-

Saloon League had nearly everything figured out except what the submerged poets and would-be Carusos were going to do with their evenings. The proletarian, often calling himself "the common dub," cannot join an expensive country club and help out on "Sweet Adeline" in the locker room. This hackneyed classic is nearly thirty years old, dating back to the later Lachrymose Period.

> "In all my dreams,
>   Your fair face beams."

This is almost a perfect specimen of the love-laden verse which was so popular in the saloons through the eighties and nineties and well into the present century. Once a prime favorite with the working classes, it is now an exclusive franchise controlled by the well-to-do. Those ominous rumblings in the ranks of organized labor come from mechanics and mill-hands, who feel that the Government had no right to take away from them not only their beer but also the chance to sing.

In one kind of place you could hear, "Wearin' of the Green," "The Harp that once through Tara's halls," "Where the River

Shannon flows," "You'll never find a coward where the shamrock grows," and that heart-searching melody which is still popular whenever or wherever four men can get their heads together, "My wild Irish Rose."

In another repository of Old World Memories the favorites might be "Hi-lee! Hilo!" "Ach du lieber Augustin," and "Die Wacht am Rhein." It was a dull evening which could not organize a Sängerfest.

But, in all of the places, during the gay nineties, when the slush-ma-gush ballads were in high favor, could have been heard the "Mother" songs and the recitals of insulted girlhood and betrayed womanhood. So far as vocal efforts were concerned, this period, which immediately pre-dated the beginning of the campaign against bar-drinking, was the saddest and most gushingly inconsequential of any in the history of the world.

It would seem that nowadays most of our popular songs are made up at the insane asylums, but a little before and after the Spanish-American War they seem to have originated either in undertaking parlors or the molasses factory.

H. T. Webster

You don't hear any "Mother" songs any more. Al Jolson pushed Mother aside and introduced "Mammy." The latter is a peculiarly Southern institution. She is a corpulent, full-breasted colored woman, with a bandanna around her head, and the only reason so many loving songs were written about her was that she knew how to cook spoon-bread and always took care of the children while mother was attending whist parties. While we are poking fun at the gummy and sticky "Mother" songs of the Saloon Days, let it be confessed that Prohibition did not improve matters very much by bursting into tears over a highly-respected negress or bursting into crooning rhapsodies over the flapperish female known as "Baby." Either she is blamed promiscuous with her hugs and kisses or else the songs are libels.

On the desk here is a great stock of the Delaney Song Books, published three times a year for many, many years, beginning about forty years ago and suspending publication only about five years ago. Probably the Delaney Co. gave up when it had to print nothing but boop-a-doop-doop and agonizing "blues." They protected their type-setters against softening of the brain by closing down.

These Delaney paper-back volumes contain the words only of songs which were in vogue and more or less admired on the various dates of publication. The early numbers are congested with tearful selections regarding "Mother." Only two songs regarding the male parent are now remembered—"Everybody works but Father" and "The Old Man's drunk again."

It was William S. Gilbert, in the policemen's song of "The Pirates of Penzance," who remarked the baffling fact that when the coster wasn't "jumping on his mother," he was addicted to harmless fun. It is a true item of history that the lazy hulk of a loafer who paid no board at home and permitted his mother to chop the wood and bring in the coal was the one who broke down and wept like a child while listening to a maudlin tribute to "dear old Mother." The saloon harbored many low-grade characters, but the least estimable of the lot was the gorilla who cried over the sentimental songs. The most gentle-hearted buccaneers were those who scuttled ships. One of the never-ending surprises of Life is that always we are finding soft-heartedness where we least expect it. Al Capone, at Miami Beach last winter, deplored the fact that the newspapers were corrupting the youth of our fair land by making it appear that gangsters and racketeers were enjoying huge profits while immune from punishment!

You might think that the saloon, established for drinking purposes, would have specialized on convivial choruses which lauded the grape or the foaming tankard, but they did not go in for anything jolly. At a college reunion or yacht club dinner you could have heard something about a "stein on the table" and "a good old snifter of Hiram Walker." The sons of toil and the mercantile slaves who flocked to the bars every evening took their pleasures seriously and wallowed in the most abject sentimentality. They liked such things as the story of the bride who was "only a bird in a gilded cage," or of "the little lost child" who found her papa, or of the indignant waitress who informed the traveling salesmen that her "mother was a lady," or of one who dwelt in "a mansion of aching hearts," or of the wayward girl whose picture had been turned "toward the wall" or of another lost soul who sent the following important message to her people:

> "Just tell them that you saw me
> And they will know the rest."

Their name was legion and all of them were weepy. They are as much out of style as low derby hats and puff sleeves but how real and beautiful they were to the emotional souses of yesterday! The ones about "Mother" predominated. Every nasal vocalist in the United States could render, "A boy's best friend is his Mother." Another was called, "Always take Mother's advice," but the real heartbreaker was, "A flower from my angel Mother's grave."

Let us rummage a little into the archives of the great Delaney and pick out a few that were typical. Even a fragment of each classic will give you some idea and help to convince you that the old-time saloon, instead of being a school for brutality, was an influence for the true, the beautiful and the good, especially about 11 p.m. with the bar-keep joining the group down near the ice-box and helping to hold the minors and the high notes.

In 1894 Dave Marion wrote one of the best, "Her eyes don't shine like diamonds," copyrighted by the Witmarks. The refrain concludes:

"With a smile she always greets me, from her I'll
    never part;
 For, lads, I love my mother and she's my sweet-
    heart."

It was in 1895 that the Witmarks published "Mother and Son," by Ellsworth. This is how the chorus started out:

"Never despair, dear mother, trust in our Father
    above,
 When you're sad, dear mother, think of your son
    and his love."

Mention has been made of the one that all of them knew, "A boy's best friend is his Mother," evidently of British origin, because it was copyrighted away back in 1883 by T. B. Harms & Company of London. The chorus was one of the best:

"Then cherish her with care and smooth her silv'ry
hair;
When gone, you will never get another;
And wherever we may turn, this lesson we will
learn—
A boy's best friend is his mother!"

Joe Flynn, remembered by some of you,
wrote "Little hoop of gold" in 1893, and it
was copyrighted by the Witmarks. It rang
with the kind of sentiment which was in fashion that year:

"Just a little band from my dear old mother's hand,
Far dearer to me now than wealth untold;
Though it's hardly worth a shilling,
Still to die I would be willing,
Ere I'd part with mother's little hoop of gold."

These were just a few of a vast assortment.
Possibly the words and music in defense of the
rights of the workingman ranked third in
popularity. First, the ones about dear old
Mother; second, the ones about the poor girl
who was tempted and who either fell or did not
fall; third, the ones about the organized work-
ingmen and their nobility of character as compared with millionaire employers. I can find
no printed copy of one I remember distinctly,

and when I print it I trust I am not disturbing
any slumbering copyright:

"Your attention, friends I'll now invite,
  While I will sing to you
  In regards to the cause of the working man
  Which, no doubt you'll find is true;
  For, the noble Knights of Labor
  Are doing the best they can
  To elevate the condition of
  The noble working man!"

In the early nineties there was a favorite
sketch in the variety halls called "Broadway
swell and Bowery bum." Willie and Eugene
Howard, of the present-day revues, have a
copy of the whole thing and will do it for you
some time, upon request. The songs and dialogue were copyrighted by Frank Harding in
1892. The Broadway swell has no friendly
greeting for the friend of former days, who is
now in tatters. The bum, quoting from Bobby
Burns, rebukes him as follows:

"Although I'm but a working man, I live by honest
    labor;
  I always do the best I can to assist a needy neigh-
    bor;

Content in health, is all my wealth, with honesty
    to back it;
My motives pure, although I'm poor, I respect a
    ragged jacket."

There you have the type of recitation which
went over with terrific success in any good
bar-room. Every regular place had a few
patrons who spouted Shakespeare and had
some smattering of the classics. Of all the
spoken pieces, probably the most popular was
the one by Burns to the effect that "A man's a
man for a' that." But there was another stand-
by which was worn threadbare before the boys
got through with it and, if you are not too
young and know the history of your country,
you have already guessed the title. No large
party, with all the faucets running, was complete without "The face on the bar-room
floor." Many a reader, when in a sentimental
and reminiscent mood, could undoubtedly recite that opening:

" 'Twas a balmy summer evening and a goodly
    crowd was there,
  Which well nigh filled Joe's bar-room, on the cor-
    ner of the square;

And as songs and witty stories came through the
open door,

A vagabond crept slowly in and posed upon the
floor."

It ran through seventeen verses and told
about the boys giving the vagabond many
drinks and of his telling the story of his life.
He had been a great artist, with a beautiful
wife, whom he adored, but a handsome young
friend stole her away and that was the beginning of his downfall. He borrows a piece of
chalk and draws her angelic likeness on the
bar-room floor and then falls over—dead! All
very dramatic and with a perfect alcoholic
finale. "The volunteer organist" and the
tragic story of the destruction of the Newhall
House in Milwaukee were in the repertoire of
every two-handed drinker who aspired to be an
elocutionist.

While we are talking about songs and reci-
tations, it is worth noting that in all the Delaney books only one song can be found which
seemed to put forward any plea for the saloon
business and that was by Edward Harrigan
and was in praise of the "Little Pitcher of
Beer." Who doesn't remember the other kind

—the songs which were directed against the "rum-shop" at every church entertainment and blue-ribbon celebration. The best remembered was the one beginning:

"Father, dear father, come home with me now,
The clock in the steeple strikes one."

Running a close second was the one about the little girl going into the saloon and singing as follows:

"Oh, Mr. Bartender, has father been here?
He's not been at home all the day—"

Then there was a scathing one called "The Drunkard's Lone Child." It certainly didn't contain any kind words for the liquor trade, and it wound up as follows:

"Dark is the night, and the storm rages wild;
God pity Bessie, the drunkard's lone child."

These selections may help you to understand that the saloons did not do all of the sobbing. For some twenty years all of the school reciters and parlor soloists and male quartets just felt that they couldn't be artistic unless they featured grief, woe, misery, death and desolation. If the old-time saloon sounded the uttermost depths of disconsolation and melancholy it was because a keg of beer contained more weeps than a whole cistern full of rainwater.

WHY SO MANY?

OUR American public has an eccentric habit of jumping from one extreme to another.

One year the whole population goes daft over the teasing perplexities of midget golf and becomes wildly excited while trying to wham the ball through hollow logs and gas-pipes and around sharp curves and over all kinds of misplaced bumps. Next year the Tom Thumb pleasure grounds are as dead as night clubs.

The popular hero is boosted to a pedestal, and then it becomes a pastime to throw dornicks at him.

Hollywood idols fade into obscurity with amazing suddenness, and the song hit which is a craze in the autumn becomes a pain in the neck before spring. Boyish bobs go out of style about the time we get used to them, and new kinds of dinky head-pieces have to be worn at startling and rakish angles. Skirts which fluttered around the knee-caps take an

134

unexpected drop, like a palsied stock market, and begin to flap around the ankles. If the soda-fountains have a run on Eskimo pie one season, they are sure to feature some fearful combination of ice-cream and syrupy fruits during the next summer. Our relatives simply will not stay put.

We raised the saloon as a pet and then gave it the chloroform.

Nearly every other country experimented around and then compromised with the liquor traffic by limiting the number of retail shops, muzzling the bars, regulating the opening and closing hours and imposing upon the trade certain strict rules intended to reduce consumption and discourage revelry. Whether or not the Gothenburg plan of Sweden and all of the post-war restrictions of Great Britain, Germany, Russia, Canada and New Zealand have promoted sobriety and improved general conditions, it is worth noting that the United States legislated to the limit against the manufacture, sale or transportation of alcoholic beverages, without any previous attempt to talk things over with the enemy or grant any terms except unconditional surrender. What is more, the Drys insist that, since Prohibition has become riveted into the Constitution, it is foolish to talk about drawing a new contract with an industry which has passed out of legal existence. Steadfast opponents of the cocktail, the high-ball and the Dutch lunch are against any attempt to deal in a friendly spirit with those Wet interests which made a joke of the law when they were supposed to be under control. These ardent Prohis cannot think of any kind of drinking at any time except in terms of the saloon. This fact is not surprising, because, right up to 1920, the old-time saloon was the flamboyant and defiant expression of all that was not so good in the booze and beer business. Wherever the saloons were tolerated they multiplied like guinea-pigs and behaved much worse.

Every one knows now that during the final years of legalized drinking, we had too many distilleries, twice too many breweries and four times too many retail establishments. Why so many? Thereby hangs a tale which some of you have forgotten, while others never heard of it. From the time of the first great inrush of German immigrants in the forties and fifties

136

of the last century, beer-drinking became popular and was generally approved as a welcome substitute for the use of native varieties of very hard liquor. The Germans not only created a demand for beer but also introduced the careful brewing methods of the Old World and turned out an enticing beverage which aroused the enthusiasm of native-born and other citizens. Beer became as much of a staple as wheat or lumber. The Rupperts and Ehrets of the East, the Moerleins of Cincinnati, the Pabst and Blatz and Schlitz families of Milwaukee, and the Busch and Lemp interests of St. Louis (to mention only a few) were careful managers, proud of their output and thorough in their organization of selling agencies. They made much money, and so imitative breweries sprang up everywhere and prices were somewhat cut and profits could not be maintained except by a constant increase of the total product.

Then along came the English syndicate to throw a monkey-wrench into the machinery and bring about a condition of affairs which helped to give the average drink-parlor a reputation as a public pest. In justice to the

British cousins, it must be said that they did not deliberately break into the brewery competition. They were lured by American slickers. The cautious investors of England had a lot of idle money and they wanted to put it into something safe that would draw down about six per cent. That rate seemed plenty high. Over here, where money was grabbed up instead of being hoarded, the speculators wanted to ride to wealth on a sky-rocket instead of climbing. The Englishman, to be sure of his income, demanded moderate dividends and a minimum of risk. The syndicate, when it took over a string of American breweries at fancy prices, appeared to be making a safe bet, because, even at the inflated valuations, it seemed certain that the profits would continue and the dividends would be ´a cinch. Most of the large concerns turned down the tempting offers of the promoters but plenty of small ones, all over the map, went into the giant merger.

Competition between the syndicate and the important beer barons became active. Both sides began to fondle the retailer and offer him tempting inducements. The average saloon

138

herb roth.

Herb Roth

THE BACK ROOM

served one make of beer and no other kind. It
received from the brewery gorgeous litho-
graphs and huge, glittering street-signs. The
better-known brands of beer were featured in
highly expensive advertising campaigns. Sales
agents found their way into every part of the
world boosting the export trade. Bill-boards
were utilized, and when I went around the
world in 1910 I saw in every country along
the beaten track reminders, on enduring metal,
that a certain kind of beer had "made Milwaukee famous."

Forcing the sale of beer became a more and
more expensive proposition. Any thriving bar-
room which switched allegiance from one brewery to another received a cut price or rebates
or some other equivalent of a cash present.
Sometimes the brewery would agree to pay
part of the rent—which was a real item for
any saloon holding down a desirable corner.
For a long time the breweries merely coddled
the saloons and granted them unusual favors.
Then the syndicate and the native beer barons
began to open their own places and furnish
them and look around for dependable partners
to officiate behind the bars. Representatives of

the English syndicate had to send dividend checks across the sea and the mammoth production plants in Jersey City, Milwaukee and St. Louis had to keep their equipment going and ship out stuff by the train-load in order to prevent a sag in the profits.

The inevitable happened. Hundreds of men without capital or much business experience were set up in business by the breweries. The new type of dealer was one who aspired to a soft living and a pleasant communion with jovial comrades without being compelled to invest any money. He started into the saloon business with nothing, so he couldn't go into the red. The brewery held a chattel mortgage on everything and expected him to dispose of so many kegs of beer each day. One heavy responsibility hung over him, and that was to get enough money to satisfy his financial backers and assure him of a continued residence on Easy Street.

New saloons were opened whenever there seemed to be a fair chance of attracting a group of bar-drinkers. They grew in number along the main thoroughfares, filtered into side streets and invaded residence districts.

142

They planted themselves next door to churches, schools and hospitals. They began to sprout in quiet neighborhoods among well-behaved homes, despite the frantic protests of property-owners and house-holders. People who wished to keep the bar-rooms within restricted areas too often found themselves up against the fact that the brewery was in friendly cahoots with the City Hall and the alderman of the ward. The saloon, although red-eyed and blowsy and of bad repute, insisted on breaking into refined circles and making the fastidious objectors like it.

It was the saloon which organized the supporters of the Anti-Saloon League. The beginning of the end was the wholesale subsidizing of irresponsible persons, who couldn't have been such lovely characters or they wouldn't have yearned so intensely to be saloon-keepers. They had to get away with near-murder in order to annex the needful amount of currency for themselves and their backers.

The beacon light over the side door at the rear lighted up the words, "Ladies' Entrance." They came in as ladies and went out pie-eyed.

143

The fuddled and irresponsible customer was permitted to keep on buying.

Tables were provided for the boys who wished to play seven-up for the drinks or who were willing to give the house a "kitty" out of each poker pot. Anything to get the coin, either in dollars or dribs.

Boys of high-school age were permitted to line up at the bar and little children brought in cans to be filled. All in line with the hoodlum idiom of the period—"Wot't'ell?"

The clock was merely a wall ornament and never indicated the closing hour as long as one spender showed a disposition to "loosen up." Sundays and holidays were simply calendar dates and were not permitted to interfere with the alleviation of thirst or the humane art of life-saving.

A consistent policy was to "fix" the "harness bull" on the beat, the theory being that any policeman who was a square guy would not bite the hand that was feeding him.

Any suggestion from a relative or employer as to cutting down the liquid rations of a regular who could not carry his load was scornfully ignored. His money was "just as good as anybody's else's," and no matter how much he wanted to mop up, that was his own affair and nobody ought to tell a good fellow where to get off.

It was a crude and barbarous code of ethics by which one kind of ruthless saloon-keeper operated his place and eased his conscience. The veteran hold-overs from the earlier period, during which drinking-places were tolerated even if they were not approved, found himself up against a new kind of competition. Many of these old-timers were not disposed to be outlaws, but they found that the daily receipts were diminishing. They had to fight the devil with fire, so they opened back rooms to provide drinking facilities for rowdy boys and girls, and were not outraged in their feelings when the moderate drinkers became heavy drinkers.

It is a weird commentary upon present distressing conditions in the United States to say that the wealthy English aristocrats who have pooh-poohed Prohibition in such sarcastic terms were responsible, perhaps innocently and indirectly, for the scandals which surrounded the retail liquor business and which

145

so worked upon public sentiment that when the Anti-Saloon League began a major attack along the whole front it attained all of the objectives and scored a bloodless victory and sat on top of the world, because those who were most familiar with the old-time saloon were not prepared to come forward with any adequate defense or any convincing alibis.

13

THE TALK

ONE of the dependables would drop in near the closing hour. You could tell by looking at him that he had been wronged. He addressed the bar-keep.

"Same as before, Fred."

"I got you, Gus. What fetches you back, after you kissin' all of us good-night?"

"Fred, you've known me for ten year— huh? Ain' that ri'?"

"All o' that, Gus."

"In all that ten year did you ever know time when ole Gus couldn't carry his licker—huh? Did you?"

"I sure never did, Gus."

"You seen me when I left here, didn't you— huh?"

"Sure."

"Listen! Wuz I cocked? Wuzn't I all ri'— huh?"

"Certainly you wuz all right—never better."

"Fred, this is jus' one frien' talkin' to 'nother. You know my wife?"

"No, Gus, I never have, but she's a lady I hear very highly spoken of."

"You're Guddimrite, Fred. She's a helva nice woman. On'y thing is she's crazy. Women ain' like men, Fred. Ever notice that? They ain' like men. Am I ri'?"

"I'll say you're right."

"Lissen! What does the ole sea gull pull on me? Huh? Git this, Fred. She says, 'What you mean comin' home 'is con'ition?' Them's the words she used, Fred. What you know 'bout that—huh?"

"She done you an injustice, Gus, but you know how women are."

"Yeah, but you don' understand, Fred. I'm a guy 'at works hard an' pulls down big money. You'd be surprise' if I told you what I done for that woman. 'What you mean comin' home 'is coni'tion?' That's a swell speech to pull on the sucker that's puttin' up for the whole works. You can' blame me for feelin' the way I do—can you, Fred?"

"Don't take it so hard, Gus. I wouldn' cry

about it if I wuz you. Everything'll be all right tomorrow."

"Wot d'ye mean every thing'll be all ri'? Wot's the big idee? Nothin'll be ri' with me till she gets down on her knees and agolo'—er—apol—er—admits she wuz wrong. Have one with me, Fred. You're the on' frien' I got left in the worl'."

"I'll take a snit. Pour it light, Gus. You got'o work tomorrow."

"Now, *you're* tellin' me wot to do, you big stiff!"

And so on.

．　　．　　．　　．　　．

The meeting of two loving pals, after a period of separation, was never so Damon and Pythias as when it came off in an old-time country saloon and was decorated with the rich vocabulary of long ago.

"Whoop-ee! Dag-gone! Gosh blame my kittens if it ain't ole Barney!"

"Well, for the good—did you ev'—? Well, I be good an' ——"

"Put 'er there, y' blamed pole-cat. Nominate your pizen!"

"You got to excuse me, Jeff, if I don't refuse. I'll take a wallop of Doctor Waldo's Scandinavian Blood Purifier."

"You're a sight for sore eyes."

"What you been doin' to yourself, Jeff? You're almost fat enough to kill."

"Been runnin' in the stalks an' I'm full o' cockle burrs. Here's hopin' your shadow'll never grow less."

"Same to you, ole stick-in-the-mud, an' may the skin of a gooseberry make overcoats fer all o' your enemies."

Enough of that. Just a cross-section of dialogue to prove that wise-cracking is not a modern invention.

．　　．　　．　　．　　．

The pest and peril of any kind of drinkshop was the "bad man." He was found in every latitude and every clime. The disorderly cow-puncher who drove his horse into the barroom and banged away at the bottles wasn't much worse than the hot-headed Southerner who wanted to protect his honor by cutting somebody into narrow strips, or the hard-faced Bowery gangster who couldn't accumulate a brannigan without setting fire to a stubborn desire to kill a policeman, or the yawping farm hand who challenged the world as soon as he was "ory-eyed." The most gilded and glittering buffets in the most exclusive city districts had just as much trouble as any one else. When the college boys and the perfect gentlemen revert to type and begin to run amuck, they are bothersome hoodlums.

Alcohol is a powerful solvent and it has a way of removing the thin veneer of civilization. The Romans had a phrase, *in vino veritas,* meaning "in wine there is truth." In other words, when a man becomes squiffy and irresponsible he has a way of saying the things that he wanted to say while he was sober. Whatever is lurking in the system comes out. He insults the people he doesn't like. His true nature emerges. If he has any baser passions or "suppressed desires," as the psycho-analysts call them, they are liberated and given full license. Look out for the well-behaved citizen who keeps himself in hand and has his fingers crossed and carefully observes the conventions, because, when he gets his nose exceedingly wet, he may want to upset tables and throw glassware.

In rural districts and along the rude frontiers there flourished a certain kind of noisy braggart who is worth remembering because of his picturesque vocabulary and vivid figures of speech. Out our way he was a corn-fed hellion with red-top boots, a red bandanna around his neck, the soiled white hat turned up in front and fastened with a tobacco tag and, if he could grow one, a cavalry moustache. When not in his cups he was merely gabby and profane but when the old essence of trouble began to steam under his belt he became a would-be combination of Frank and Jesse James, the Dalton boys and "Wild Bill" Hickok. Blue smoke curled from the nostrils and he just had to fight some one. He was a sore trial to any bar-keep.

"I can outwrassle, outrun or outfight any skunk in this here town, an' don't you forgit 'er!" was the manner in which he proclaimed himself. "Any gent present that don't like the cut o' my jib kin git satisfaction by steppin' up to the captain's office. That goes double fer these town dudes."

All of this apropos of nothing and just for advertising purposes. Then Bill, back of the bar, would try to calm him down: "Look here, Bud, them boys down at the end o' the bar are all friends o' mine an' they ain't botherin' you none, so you jes' quile down an' leave 'em alone."

"I can lick all three of 'em with one hand tied behind me. Them's what I eat fer breakfast. I'm a prairie wolf an' this is my day to howl. I'm chain lightnin' an' nobody'd better fuss with me. I'm a bad man from the head waters o' Bitter Creek. I eat raw meat an' drink blood. I'm poison ivy an' don't tech me. I'm long an' wooly an' full o' fleas an' I never wuz curried below the knees. I got two rows o' nipples an' holes bored for more. I'm bad news. I pull up trees by the roots an' if a mountain gits in my way, I jes' kick her to one side. I'm a rarin', tarin', rootin', tootin', rip-snortin' cyclone an' jes' loaded 'ith destruction. I'm walkin' on both sides o' the street today an' nobody'd better git in my way. I'm the ory boryalis an' I fill the northern sky. Whoopee! Yip, yip! That's ole Bud fer you— the idol o' the women an' the envy o' the men."

153

These defiant rigamaroles of worthless blow-hards were in general circulation and highly prized. Sometimes the dreadful combination of cyclone, prairie wolf and aurora borealis found the battle he was looking for and got a billiard cue over the head or a beer keg in the pit of the stomach. More often he was permitted to vapor. If he became too much of a nuisance the town marshal might be compelled to slap his face and lead him away to the lock-up.

It was the brash and insolent talk which so many customers babbled when John Barleycorn had a strangle hold on them that led up to the continual fighting in saloons. It is significant that the kind of personal encounter which ignored all the rules of fair play and involved "the boots," gouging, biting, or the use of any weapon that could be grabbed up, was definitely and generally known as "bar-room fighting." If the word "bar-room" became a synonym for something savage and uncivilized it was because the old-time saloon was too often a den of beasts instead of a "hall or apartment set aside for social intercourse and a free discussion of the arts and sciences."

14

EXPLAINING
SOME MYSTERIES

"FUNNY thing about Rupert Hemingway. Before Prohibition he wouldn't touch a thing and now he goes after a cocktail like a trout after a fly."

You've heard that so often you're tired of listening. And, in these days of distressful problems, when every one is busy shooing the wolf away from the front stoop, who has time to brood over the fact that Mr. Hemingway, once a frigid abstainer, is now a gay and larksome partaker?

The stereotyped and shelf-worn explanation of the fact that many teetotalers are now moderate tipplers is that the sipping of an illegal cocktail is spiced with adventure. The casual flirters with the Demon Rum resent the attempt of the Government to stop them from doing something they never did and never wanted to do. They are told they mustn't do this or do that, so they lay back their ears and

155

go ahead and do all of the things forbidden,
just to prove that they are unshackled freemen
and no one can tell them where to get off.
Now, that is about the only popular explanation of the phenomenon of non-drinkers becoming drinkers as soon as every convivial
party degenerated into a round-up of semi-
criminals.

Here is a new explanation and probably the
correct one. The gay practice of lifting an
occasional snifter acquired social status and
lost many of its horrid aspects just as soon as
the serving of drinks was transferred from the
old-time saloon to the attractive and cozy and'
tastefully decorated American Home. The
bar-room was banished because it had persistently made enemies and was shunned by the
"nice people." But these same nice people
didn't have any abiding prejudice against the
homes of their friends.

You remember a mention of those four
saloons in our little country town. Any man
seen entering one of those doggeries was
doomed to local ostracism. He just the same
as burned his Methodist clothes and joined the
leper colony. Many and many a customer

sauntered up a deserted alley and then ducked suddenly into a boarded-up chute leading to the back door and then had a drink brought out to him secretively, because he didn't want to mingle with the trash hanging around the bar. Taking a drink seemed to be about as reprehensible as burning an orphan asylum. Some of the steady lushers made arrangements with the drug stores and others, who thought they were deluding themselves, swigged bottle after bottle of some proprietory "tonic," with a medicinal label, which wasn't anything in the world except a low grade of whisky with some sweetening and enough bitters to give it a puckery taste. I can recall many a foe of the rum-shop, wearing throat whiskers and one of our best little hymn singers, who bought his tonic six quarts at a time because it seemed to help "that run-down feeling."

Anyway, the village patron of the old-time saloon was supposed to be without shame and lost to all sense of decency. The godly residents wagged their heads at him and the women and girls avoided him as a wild and dangerous character.

In the college town where I continued my

study of the retail liquor traffic, the drinking person had a somewhat better chance to escape utter disgrace but he was not encouraged to be proud of his moral delinquencies. Our best-known bar, enjoying the patronage of well known residents, was in a wing of the principal hotel, but it was significant that most of the customers did not go in from the broad daylight of Fifth Street, but strolled through the hotel lobby and angled off toward a dim corridor, trying to act as if they might be heading for the wash-room to have their shoes shined. They knew that everybody knew that they nipped or guzzled once in a while but, possibly because of a hold-over from early training, they didn't care to blazon the news every time a drink was hoisted. Many of the students from the University were enthusiastic beer-drinkers and probably four-fifths of them at some time or other in their college careers drank sparingly of the popular beverage. They were not interested in hard liquor and carried no flasks and the cautious ones, even when partaking of beer, sought the quiet German places on the side streets. They had a wholesome fear of faculty spies. The boy caught drinking at a

158

bar was suspended or expelled, unless his previous record was clean and he begged hard and promised to reform. Any undergraduate who appeared at a dance or a campus celebration in a lit-up condition scandalized himself, because the co-eds were non-drinkers, and marked off their lists the desperados who advertised their bad habits.

Even in the lârger cities a good proportion of the moderate drinkers and many of the steady consumers were shame-faced about loitering in saloons. They chewed roasted coffee and sucked cloves in order to avert suspicion on the part of relatives or business associates. A lot of drinking went on, but much of it was artfully concealed and the plain fact is that any man known to be a confirmed bar-drinker lost caste, if he had any to lose.

We must consider the widespread ill-repute of the old-time saloon to understand why certain baffling conditions showed up soon after the open retail liquor shops were wiped out of existence. The cocktail, even after it became an illegal concoction, acquired a surprising respectability because it was no longer in odious partnership with disreputable resorts. No

159

woman with a vestige of social rating ever went near the regulation old-time saloon. The well-behaved rathskellers and popular restaurants in which beverages were served at the tables could be found only in the cities. Ostensibly, they went out of business with the saloons. Some of them tried to cheat the new restrictions for a while, but you know that practically all of them closed up eventually and the drinking, if any, was transferred to the speak-easies, to hotel bed-rooms, hidden nooks in private clubs, adventurous soft-drink parlors and the homes of people who could manage to pay boot-leg prices.

These are the plain facts, and will be admitted by the most perplexed and indignant Dry.

If you read the blanket dailies published in the larger cities you will get a lot of amazing information about "speak-easies." There may be thousands of them, as reported. I am like Bill Rogers. All I know is what I read in the papers. I hope to die if I have ever seen the inside of one of these hole-in-the-door and a dollar a throw imitations of the old-time saloon. I am Dun and Bradstreet on the various kinds

160

of bar-room that bloomed so freely in the Garden of Dissipation when I was out in the world, finding out about things, but I am a doddering ignoramus regarding the new type of under-cover resort. I do know that if "speak-easy" means a place in which conversation is hushed and subdued, it bears no resemblance to the old-time saloon. These high-priced parlors which cannot be entered until the customer has given the sign and pass-word and shown his bank-roll are not to be found except in the centers of population, but the outlaw defiance of the great Amendment and the Volstead Act may be found everywhere, even to the most outlying townships.

The woman who never went near a boisterous bar-room or sat in a restaurant which sent drinks to the table, and the man who didn't like to find himself in any kind of a boozing den, do not know how to refuse a cocktail when it is proffered by a prominent executive in a dinner jacket or a charming hostess in an evening frock.

If Prohibition has not accomplished the wonders that were promised, possibly it is because the consumption of high-balls in the locker room and the absorption of gin and orange juice in the drawing room, now have the modernistic environment and background and an enveloping glamour which the old-time saloon failed to provide.

Whether the reader of these lines happens to be a die-in-the-last-ditch Prohi, or, as I am, a member of the Association Against the Eighteenth Amendment and the Volstead Act, he or she will admit that the drinking habits of the gay, motor-riding, jazz-dancing, recklessly-necking youngsters who have come from the cradle and up through the nursery since 1920, are pretty deplorable. The boys and girls now in their late teens are more sophisticated and better specimens of physical development and more sensibly attired and better-groomed than the yappy youngsters of the eighties and nineties. They raise Cain all of the time and yet, for some reason, there are fewer shot-gun marriages than there used to be in the prairie towns of the primeval eighties and nineties. We are surrounded by new and astounding complications. The high school students and the collegians have been shown up in countless magazine articles and novels and picture shows as hoop-la night riders and hell-raisers in general. "Flaming youth" is the most hackneyed of all topics. It has been worn thread-bare and put under the ban. And yet, these same incorrigible kids are first-class athletes when we see them in swimming matches or playing football, basket-ball and tennis, or breaking records in track meets. The old-time saloon never had a chance to exert an evil influence over any one of them. Why do they act up? They may not be as bad as painted, but there is no question as to some of them being painted. They have gleefully adjusted themselves to a brand-new set of conditions and accepted the well-known advice to "live dangerously." Not wet—not dry—just history.

15

''DIDN'T HE RAMBLE?''

LEGEND has it that, at about the beginning
of the present century, a vagabond goat, of
most bedraggled appearance and with the up-
holstery worn off at every corner, ranged
through the alleys and by-ways of the red-
light district of Chicago. He was tolerated
and humored and indulged. He had many
feeding places on his route. The police hod-
nobbed with him and permitted him to butt
small boys off the sidewalk. He was living in
a goat's paradise, the happy pet of wild women
and midnight rounders. He was perfectly adjusted to his environment.

One day a flock of sheep came along 22nd
Street and the goat fell in with his cousins,
saying to himself: "I'll stick along. This looks
like a big party somewhere."

He didn't believe that he had an enemy in
the world or that any one would interfere
with the routine of his care-free existence.

So he rambled along with the gang, south

on Halsted Street, bleating cheerfully, and presently he found himself in a long chute, with the crowd pushing from behind. He could not turn back. Being a natural-born goat he made no attempt to escape. Impelled by that spirit of curiosity which is the only redeeming trait of all goats, human and otherwise, he passed into a slaughter-house. Next day, goat was being served for mutton, and a true sport was missing from the favorite haunts.

The story of his tragic fate traveled around and a song was written about him. George Primrose made the song popular. It became a favorite at every college. Bob Cole, of the talented colored team of Cole and Johnson, is said to have written the song about 1904, and the copyright was renewed in 1921 by the Marks Music Co. The refrain was as follows:

"Oh, didn't he ramble, ramble?
He rambled all around,
In and out of the town;
Oh, didn't he ramble, ramble?
He rambled 'till the butcher cut him down."

That's the text for this delayed funeral sermon over the remains of the old-time saloon, "Oh, didn't he ramble?" He rambled into politics and down to the City Hall. He rambled into suburbs and away out into the country lanes. He rambled into residence districts and exclusive subdivisions, and wherever he rambled he took with him an air of abject unworthiness and a penetrating aroma. He rambled into the factory districts to such an extent that every workman going home with the precious pay envelope had to pass about twenty dingy resorts, each of them beckoning for him to enter. He wandered into every small town and city precinct which offered the slightest prospect of business. He rambled into the cemetery entrances, so that the mourners and pall-bearers could find immediate solace and comfort after taking off their cotton gloves and other emblems of woe. He wagged his fuzzy tail and made ribald noises on every street traversed by college students and the white collared armies employed by jobbing houses and large department stores. He rambled along every highway except the straight and narrow path of obedience to the law and a strict adherence to civilized methods.

The goat in the parable could not understand why any one should drive him up a

166

shute and tap him on the head with a sledge hammer. The average low-brow saloon-keeper could not believe that he was headed for destruction. He didn't worry until the butcher cut him down—and then it was too late to enter a protest.

There had been a time when the drink-shops simply served people who came in and faced the bar. Before they were put out of business, so keen was the competition, they roped prospective customers and, on Saturday afternoon, tried to beat the wife and children to the pay envelope. They got in wrong with the railway companies, the steel mills, every sort of factory and every kind of mercantile establishment. The retail liquor traffic took an awful beating in 1920 because it had been on the loose for a long time, had no organized defense and very few friends who dared to show up in court.

When you stand on top of a hill and view, in fair perspective, the Rise and Fall of the Old-Time Saloon, you will admit that this aforesaid institution doesn't seem to have much of a chance of staging a come-back and resuming business on a large scale.

167

The provinces of Canada discarded Prohibition as a failure, but they did not tolerate the return of any retail establishment in which drinks were pushed over the bar. When they revised their laws they abolished the "pubs," in spite of the fact that these places had been more orderly and law-abiding than the Yank saloons across the border.

The bigoted and extreme Drys haven't helped their cause any by being so dour and bitter and dogmatic and cruel in their judgments. They insist that any man or woman who believes that the 18th Amendment and the Volstead Act have team-worked together to produce a spectacular fizzle, is inwardly in favor of a saloon in every block. They say, in spite of what is going on in Canada, that if we legalize any kind of drinking we must have open bars. All of the organizations which are trying to bring about the repeal of the Amendment and the Act have it written in their platforms that they are against the old-time saloon. Whereupon the Drys insist, "You say it but you don't mean it."

No doubt some person, somewhere, who sincerely demands a continuance of all Prohibi-

tion enactments, just because he believes that
people shouldn't drink anything, will dip into
this harmless and good-natured little volume
and discover that it is a defense or a plea in
mitigation of the old-time saloon. This kind
of reformer is too rabid. He will not admit
that the licensed drink-shop had a certain entertainment value and helped to give color to
an old-fashioned era, now in the dim past. His
mission on earth seems to be to demonstrate
the fact that one who is extremely righteous
cannot be companionable. The whole liquor
traffic was abolished by an indignant majority
because the saloons were defiant of the law,
would not discuss any compromise and could
not speak of their opponents except in terms
of violent abuse. The ultra-Drys have had
their day in court, and now they are in danger
of getting on the nerves of those who do not
happen to absolutely agree with them. They
are so militant in their goodness that they at-
tribute the basest motives to all opponents.
They should remember that the American
public will not stand for intolerance, in the
long run, and that it has a way of jumping

from one extreme to another, as already suggested.

If anybody has discovered in this write-up of the old-time saloon any arguments in favor of re-opening those hundreds and hundreds of beer fountains and booze parlors, he has read between the lines something which isn't there.

The best reason for believing that bar-drinking will never again be an approved indoor sport is that the old-time saloon was abolished by a powerful combination of enemies most of whom still nurse their hatreds, while the organized wets have a definite grievance against the kind of reckless retailing that aroused public sentiment and gave a wide opening for the Anti-Saloon League.

Why did this League acquire such a sudden and overwhelming importance and put through its drastic program without a hitch or a delay?

In the first place, the war propaganda had not been friendly to the making of any drinks which called for the use of grain, the combustion of coal, the employment of labor and the use of railway cars for transportation. The Anti-Saloon League had the Liquor Business

170

under the ether, so it said, "Why not slip him an overdose and let him remain dead forever?"

Who supplied the additional ether? The millionaire church members who were sternly opposed to any kind of drinking. They are the ones mainly responsible for the 18th Amendment and the Volstead Act. They and the railway officials and captains of industry and merchant princes who employed thousands and thousands of men, and who believed that these men would be more efficient and capable, speeding up production and increasing sales, if we could just pass some laws making it impossible for any hired hand to get a drink at any time. The Rockefellers, John Wanamaker, Mrs. Russell Sage, Mr. Kresge, of the chain stores, and Mr. Candler, soft-drink monarch of Atlanta, were among the early and heavy contributors. Prohibition was no longer advocated as a moral uplift but as an economic necessity. Mr. Wheeler was given all the money he needed. He applied pressure to Senators and Congressmen and all the little legislators in all the scattered states. He threatened them with defeat at the polls if they ignored the church vote and the woman

171

vote. While they were eating out of his hand, no one came near any one of these law-makers to plead for the old-time saloon and the industries it represented.

It is true that the orthodox Protestant churches were against the saloons and always had been. They helped to put on the big show. Undoubtedly the women whose husbands had been wasting their wages and salaries at the corner places cherished a bitter hatred of saloons in general. Then there were the parents, not all of them abstainers, who didn't want their boys to be subject to the allurements and temptations of the gaudy barrooms.

Most of the millionaires no longer contribute to the League. Church opinion is now somewhat divided. The women, who were supposed to be solidly against the accursed traffic, are acting strangely. When Col. "Jim Ham" Lewis, running as a Wet candidate in Illinois, ran up a plurality of away over a half-million, it came out in the returns that the women voted anti-Prohibition in about the same proportion as the men. As for the American parents who believed that the closing of the old-time saloons would result in the removal of all temptations surrounding boys (and girls), it would be a plain perversion of history to deny that they are somewhat flabbergasted by recent developments.

But—and this is important—of all those individuals who welcomed the sweeping legislation in 1920, not one has changed his private opinion of the conventional saloon of the wide-open period, even though he or she may begin to suspect that the prescribed remedies have not effected a satisfactory cure.

You remember some black sheep of your family tribe, long since banished from the circle of respected relatives, and sometimes you chuckle over his amusing misdeeds and at other times you realize that time has softened your former harsh judgments, but, just the same, you do not send for him to come back and live with you.

When we collect our memories of the old-time saloon we see a flushed person, somewhat overweight from flabbishness, the hat cocked over one eye, the breath spicy, the manner effusive, the morals uncertain and the wardrobe not distinguished by quiet elegance. We may get together once in a while and talk about the dear departed and his antics and laugh over the many social errors he committed and the trouble he kicked up, but who in the dickens wants to re-incarnate him and turn him loose again?

Harrison Fisher

OH, YES?

NOTES

Due to space constraints, I have made some choices. First, since this is a popular history, no footnotes; sources for historical facts cited can be found among the texts listed in the bibliography at the end of this volume, and when a specific note can be elucidated by a particular source, I cite it in the note by the author's last name. As for the idiosyncratic opinions, random speculations, and wild theories: those are all mine. Second, I do not provide birth and death dates for historical personages, because some of Ade's references were too obscure to reliably verify, while others are easily available online. Unless otherwise stated, all famous or obscure public figures Ade mentions were drinking in, or fighting against, saloons from roughly1880 to 1930.

Bill Savage
Chicago, 2016

Page iii
The identities of the "Chosen Few" who Ade thought would "Understand" on November 10, 1931, are unknown. The teardrop, though, could also be seen as a spilled drop of bootleg hooch. This new edition is published for the Chosen Many who are Interested in American saloon history.

Page xii
Ade's illustrators constitute a canon of American popular cartooning and illustration.

NOTES

REA IRVIN. One of the founders of the *New Yorker*. His most famed drawing is that magazine's iconic Eustace Tilley.

GLUYAS WILLIAMS. Produced book covers as well as cartoons for magazines such as the *New Yorker* and *Cosmopolitan*. Early in the twentieth century, *Cosmopolitan* featured political exposés, urban slice-of-life stories, and quality fiction.

JOHN HELD, JR. His jazzy cartoons of flappers and their suitors defined an image of 1920s Prohibition culture. His linocuts often satirized the then-recent Victorian past.

JAMES MONTGOMERY FLAGG. Created one of American culture's most enduring images with his Uncle Sam "I Want YOU for US Army" recruiting poster in 1916–17.

LEON GORDON. A pen name of Leonard Dworkins, who drew syndicated daily cartoon strips, including "Buck Rogers."

R. L. GOLDBERG. A.k.a. Rube Goldberg. A prolific artist who had an engineering degree and is most famed for his comic illustrations of elaborate contraptions designed for simple tasks.

H. T. WEBSTER. His comic strip "The Timid Soul" starred Caspar Milquetoast, whose name has joined the American lexicon as a spineless someone who (as Webster described him) "speaks softly and gets hit with a big stick."

HERB ROTH. A cartoonist and Webster's assistant.

HARRISON FISHER. A cover artist for *Cosmopolitan* and the *Saturday Evening Post*. He was most renowned for his drawings of fashionable women. His sketch of a bartender on page 175 of this volume bears a remarkable resemblance to Ernest

Hemingway, perhaps not coincidentally. Fisher's portrait of F. Scott Fitzgerald resides in the National Portrait Gallery.

Page 1

ANTI-SALOON LEAGUE . . . W. C. T. U. Both Evangelical Christian organizations were dedicated to ridding America of alcohol, but the Anti-Saloon League (ASL) is largely forgotten while the WCTU lives on. The ASL achieved its goals by electing politicians who would get the Eighteenth Amendment passed in Congress and ratified by the states. The WCTU pre-dated the ASL, but its wider progressive focus on women's rights and suffrage, as well as its female leadership, made it less central to the achievement of Prohibition. It survives in the twenty-first century, still fighting for abstinence and other evangelical causes. The ASL, its cause now lost, lingers on as the American Council on Addiction and Alcohol Problems, dedicated to personal temperance and restrictions on alcohol advertising. The ASL's archive in the public library of Westerville, Ohio, is well worth visiting, as is the Frances E. Willard House Museum and Archives in Evanston, Illinois.

Ade takes for granted that his readers knew about the politics of Prohibition, but for contemporary readers one key question remains. As Daniel Okrent put it: "How the hell did that happen?" How did the fifth-largest industry in the United States, encompassing many thousands of jobs and participated in at every social level by millions of people, become illegal? How could there be a political argument where Jane Addams and the Ku Klux Klan were both on the same side, in favor of prohibiting alcohol?

Prohibition can be understood as an argument over American identity. Supporters of Prohibition, Drys, tended to be rural or small town, white "native" Americans, Protestant, and largely female (especially the leadership, from the over-the-top Carrie Nation to progressive feminist stalwarts like Frances E. Willard). Their Wet opponents tended to be urban, with immigrant origins, and Catholic or Jewish. Nelson Algren described this division as between "the Do-as-I-Sayers and the Live-and-Let-Livers." The original antialcohol movement, in the early nineteenth century, was about personal temperance (individuals trying to drink less); it evolved to promote total abstinence (swearing to not drink at all). But many Americans abstained from abstaining, and so the ardent Drys eventually fought to ban alcohol altogether. Unless the temptation of the saloon was eliminated, they believed, America would continue to drown in drink. Other aspects of American culture came into play: anti-German prejudice in the lead-up to the Great War combined with astute political organization won the day. Drys also benefited from the passage of the Sixteenth Amendment; the new income tax allowed the federal government to function without excise tax revenue from liquor. See Okrent; McGirr.

HOSTETTER'S BITTERS. An herbal "health tonic" which contained alcohol.

Page 4

18TH AMENDMENT. The amendment that prohibited "the manufacture, sale, or transportation of intoxicating liquors within, the importation thereof into, or the exportation thereof from the United States." It was the first amendment to the US Constitution that expanded government power rather than guaranteeing personal rights.

VOLSTEAD ACT. The Eighteenth Amendment expressed a lofty ideal, but it had to be translated into enforceable law. That law was written by Wayne Wheeler, chief of the Anti-Saloon League, and sponsored by Minnesota US Representative Andrew Volstead.

RESORT. Any place where people congregated outside of home, work, or church. Barber shops, restaurants, parks, racetracks, and theaters would also be considered "resorts." Sociologist Ray Oldenburg has dubbed such locations the "third place." After home and work—first and second places, respectively—people need a third place where they can form community based on shared interests and concerns, rather than kinship or economic forces. See Oldenburg; Powers; Dunbar.

Page 5

ARNICA. A genus of aromatic plants, some of which were used in alcohol-based patent medicines like Hostetter's Bitters.

Page 6

"CONFESSIONS OF AN ILL-SPENT LIFE." Ade indeed frequented saloons. His depictions of rural and small-town bar culture come from his hometown Kentland, Indiana, and the West Lafayette, Indiana, area, where he attended Purdue University. His experiences as a reporter in Chicago and a Broadway playwright and world traveler provide the rest.

KENTUCKY SOUR MASH. A variety of bourbon whiskey.

Page 8

PORT SAID . . . NEW ORLEANS. Cities famed for their vice districts.

THE LOOP. Chicago's central business area and the location of countless saloons before Prohibition, with lesser numbers during and after the Dry period.

A BLARING . . . RED-LIGHT DISTRICT. Ade might be referring to any one of several such areas, but the Levee, south of the Loop, was the most infamous, teeming with bars, opium dens, gambling houses, and brothels ranging from horrific cribs to the opulent Everleigh Club.

PITCH-AND-TOSS. A game of chance in which players toss coins at a mark.

Page 11

PROBABLY NO OTHER CITY. For people around the world, Chicago epitomized the gang warfare of bootleggers. While such violence was a nationwide fact, Chicago's Al Capone was a publicity hound who became the scarred face of the rackets. Chicago's newspapers, along with writers like Ben Hecht, helped to romanticize organized crime. See Eig.

Page 12

EVE OF THE GREAT EXPOSITION. The 1933 Century of Progress International Exposition.

Page 13

VAGS. Vagrants; homeless men.

THE BADGER GAME OR THE USE OF CHLORAL HYDRATE. Cons perpetrated on unwary or foolish pleasure-seeking men by confidence women and their male partners. In the badger game, a woman would lure a man to her room and then a male confederate would appear to rob, or later blackmail, the victim. Chloral hydrate (knockout drops) were more direct: the woman would rob her unconscious paramour after drugging his drink. Mickey Finn, proprietor of the Lone Star Saloon and Palm Garden on South State Street, lent his name to this sort of drink.

SODOM AND GOMORRAH. Cities of the Plain, synonymous with wickedness and so destroyed by a vengeful God. See *Genesis 19*.

HOP-JOINTS. Opium dens.

Page 14

FROM THE COUNTRY. Ade had retired from newspapering to an estate in Indiana.

RIP VAN WINKLE. The title character in an 1819 Washington Irving tale. He misses the American Revolution after drinking and bowling with some mysterious ghosts in the Catskill Mountains; their otherworldly liquor knocks him out for twenty years.

Page 15

JOHN MCCUTCHEON. Fellow Purdue graduate and Sigma Chi, McCutcheon illustrated Ade's columns. He won the Pulitzer Prize for editorial cartooning in 1932.

LAW-ABIDING GERMANS. Germans were Chicago's largest immigrant group, and many lived in Old Town, north of the Chicago River, far from various vice districts.

SICILIAN. Gangsters of many ethnicities manned the bootlegging front lines, though Al Capone helped create the stereotype of the Italian gangster. Before Prohibition, urban American organized criminals preyed on their fellow immigrants with protection rackets, gambling, and vice. Prohibition gave the more enterprising of these marginalized gangs the opportunity to expand their customer base beyond their countrymen, and so they made vast fortunes and founded criminal enterprises that endure into the twenty-first century.

Page 17

ON THE BRASS RAIL. One signature feature of the old-time saloon. Many saloons had no stools; men sat at tables or stood at the bar, and the brass rail made standing more comfortable.

Page 18

LOCAL OPTION. Federal law had long allowed local governments to regulate or prohibit alcohol. Before 1919, many neighborhoods, cities, and states were already legally dry.

Page 20

WAYNE B. WHEELER. The political, oratorical, and organizational genius behind the success of the Anti-Saloon League. See Okrent; McGirr.

WOODROW WILSON. President of the United States when the Eighteenth Amendment was passed.

Page 23

RAINES LAW. Passed in 1896, this law required any saloon open on Sunday to have ten rooms, not one. That requirement led, as morals laws often did, to unintended consequences, as saloons were then even more likely to be sites for prostitution or other assignations.

Page 26

THE NON-DRINKERS. Ade here proves that all-caps, bold typography is the equivalent of shouting long before the evolution of online social media.

HOFFMAN HOUSE BAR . . . "ED" STOKES. The infamous Stokes (he served four years in Sing-Sing for shooting a rival whose mistress he'd had an affair with) co-owned the opulent bar in the Hoffman House Hotel, on Broadway between 24th and 25th Streets. The bar featured an enormous painting, *Nymphs and Satyr*, that scandalized the easily scandalized.

Page 27

KNICKERBOCKER DRINKING PARLOR. Beaux-Arts hotel at the corner of 42nd and Broadway. It hosted such luminaries as Enrico Caruso and George M. Cohan. The hotel bar featured a huge mural by Maxfield Parrish, and the bar's popularity led to its "forty-second street country club" nickname. The lyrics to Cohan's "Give My Regards to Broadway" refer to it:

> Give my regards to Broadway
> Remember me to Herald Square
> Tell all the gang at Forty-Second Street
> That I will soon be there

SAZERAC OR RAMOS . . . WALDORF. The "Ramos" gin fizz was (and is) the signature cocktail of the New Orleans Sazerac Hotel Bar. The other establishments Ade lists here were (or are) all high-end hotel resorts, frequented by the securely well-to-do and social climbers alike.

Page 28

SHUTTERED. Some cities passed laws after Prohibition requiring that bars have unobscured windows to give bargoers the sense that their behavior is being observed by the community so they would behave properly. Ironically, other cities required bars to have their windows blacked out to prevent people on the street from being enticed into the place by the sight of people having fun.

POTTED FERNS. An ironic historic detail, as the term "fern bar" in the 1970s and 1980s meant an upscale and/or pretentious joint that tried to attract a female and female-seeking yuppie clientele with décor including potted ferns and other "feminine" touches.

Page 31

FORTY-ROD T.N.T. A very strong drink. A "rod" is an archaic English measure of distance equal to 5.5 yards; 40 rods would be 220 yards. TNT, of course, is dynamite.

Page 32

FOOTLIGHT FAVORITES . . . PRIZE FIGHTERS. Saloons often featured "odalisques" or other risqué paintings or photographs of famed actresses and athletes. Ade's joke reminds us that the beauty standards which men impose on women come and go and come back again. The presumably white and Confederate Kentucky Colonel here might have more in common with African American rapper Sir Mix-a-Lot of "Baby Got Back" renown than any gender or racial theorist might predict.

JOHN L. SULLIVAN . . . THE BOSTON STRONG BOY. Famed boxer, last of the bare-knuckle London Prize Ring Rules champions, and first Heavyweight World Champion of the modern age. A noted drinker, brawler, and bar owner, Sullivan repented and promoted temperance. As a reporter, Ade covered the controversial Sullivan-Corbett fight of 1892, in which Jim Corbett upset Sullivan.

Page 34

THE FREE LUNCH. All sorts of saloons provided free food to customers who purchased a drink, and no aspect of saloon culture evoked more divergent responses. The poor saw free lunches as a blessing, even a necessity. Many industrial plants didn't provide cafeteria or lunchroom services, but in the saloon across from the factory gates, if you had a nickel, you not only got a beer, you got some substantial food to fuel your after-lunch labor. In a society with no government public assistance for the long-term poor or the temporarily unemployed, the free lunch could be understood as a form of social welfare. Drys disagreed, as negative depictions of the free lunch from muckrakers such as Upton Sinclair, in *The Jungle*, show. The Drys saw the free lunch as an enticement to get working class men to waste their hard-earned money on drink, enriching bar owners, distillers, and brewers at the expense of wives and children. Ade seems to side with the Drys here, satirizing the assumption that such lunches were luxurious or posh or even nutritious rather than utilitarian and salty enough to get drinkers to spend more.

DELMONICO AND SHERRY. Deluxe New York restaurants.

Page 36

HIT THE GRIT. Archaic slang for hobos who have fallen, or been pushed, out of a rail car, and so "hit the grit" of the gravel railbed.

NOTES

Page 37

ARGUS-EYED. In Greek mythology, Argus was an all-seeing watchman.

BUNG STARTER. The hammer with which a wooden keg of beer would have its sealed bunghole pierced so it could be tapped and served. A handy improvised weapon as well. See p. 29.

See p. 29.

Page 38

A LOSS OF TWENTY YARDS. Ade was an ardent college football fan; the football stadium at his alma mater Purdue University is named Ross-Ade Stadium to honor the fundraising of Ade and fellow alum David Ross. For those unfamiliar with American football, a loss of twenty yards would be a serious setback.

NEW YORK HIPPODROME. On Sixth Avenue between 43rd and 44th Streets, the Hippodrome was an opulent theater seating 5,300 and capable of hosting entire circuses.

Page 41

MALACHY HOGAN. In December of 1898, the *Chicago Tribune* reported—shockingly!—that Hogan's saloon at 75 North Clark also hosted gambling.

Page 42

COLLECTOR OF PORT RUSSELL. Martin Russell was named Collector for the Port of Chicago, a lucrative patronage position, by President Cleveland.

ARCHBISHOP FEEHAN. Chicago's first Roman Catholic archbishop.

MAGGIE CLINE. Irish-American singer and vaudevillian.

Page 43

McVICKER THEATRE BUILDING. From 1857 to 1984, various incarnations of McVicker (or McVicker's) occupied the southeast corner of Madison and Dearborn.

Page 44

SARDELLEN. German for "anchovy."

"BIFF" HALL . . . TURN-OVER CLUB. William "Biff" Hall, a prominent actor, led the Turn-Over Club, which was exclusively for theater people. This reference, and others, demonstrates the close relationship between saloons and night life, entertainment, and leisure culture.

Page 46

LUCULLUS. Roman general and patron of the arts and sciences in the late period of the Republic.

"DIAMOND JIM" BRADY. Gilded Age businessman renowned for his prodigious appetite.

Page 49

POUSSE CAFÉ. A multi-ingredient cocktail that requires painstaking care when being poured so the liquids settle into visibly distinct layers based on the specific gravities of the ingredients.

ABSINTHE. A French spirit with allegedly hallucinogenic properties, traditionally served after being precisely dripped over a spoon of sugar into water.

Page 50

"JACK ROSE." A cocktail made with applejack brandy, grenadine, lemon juice, and bitters.

NOTES

Page 51

MEASURED. Arguments continue over whether to precisely measure liquor as it is served. Some drinkers and barkeeps want precision for every ingredient in a complex cocktail, while others favor the more liberal (i.e., stronger) free pour. As Ade suggests just below, doggeries didn't just free pour, they handed out the bottle and a glass and the customer poured for himself.

Page 55

BARREL-HOUSES AND OUT-AND-OUT JOINTS. Lower-class saloons that did not feature any music or entertainment and where empty liquor barrels might serve as tables for the stand-up customers. Samuel Paynter Wilson, in *Chicago and Its Cess-Pools of Infamy*, writes, "The 'barrel-houses' are located in the poorer sections of the city where the liquors of the vilest kind are sold. Their customers are the poor and wretched" (145).

Page 56

NOT TO DRINK YOUR LIQUOR STRAIGHT WAS CONSIDERED A SIGN OF EFFEMINACY. This statement is especially interesting since Ade was quite probably gay.

The evidence is circumstantial, but in an era where the closet was more commodious than many other rooms, lack of evidence is not surprising. Ade never married and for many years kept close company and traveled the world with another man, Orson "Ort" Welles. Their relationship was common knowledge, as evidenced by a painting that hung in Chicago's Chapin and Gore saloon. It depicts Ade and Welles in Egypt (where they had traveled together), with Welles wearing clothes then coded queer and Ade in a dress. Other portraits in the bar satirized famous figures like Daniel Burnham, but only openly queer Oscar Wilde, Mary Walker (a female surgeon who dressed in men's clothes and who had won a Medal of Honor in the Civil War), and Welles and Ade were depicted in ways that questioned their gender. When Welles died in 1939, Ade came out of journalistic retirement to write his obituary. His editor at the *Daily News* presumably wrote the subhead describing this piece as "A Labor of Love." This phrase could be read two ways, of course: returning to the labor Ade loved, writing for the papers; or writing up the life of a man he loved.

However complicated Ade's gender identity might have been, the gender politics of his vision of the saloon are straightforward: it was a man's space. Ade depicts women in saloons, but only in patriarchal terms. Women are either saintly (mothers, daughters, Salvation Army do-gooders) or evil (prostitutes). In Ade's saloons, men sing sentimentally about their mothers, or "painted women" engage in sexual commerce.

This book suggests that, for Ade, being a man was not just defined by sexuality, but by manly public performance, including how one drank among other men in the saloon. Ade suggests that a man's masculinity depends not on whether he is gay or straight, but on whether he drinks his whiskey straight.

SCOFFLAWS. A term coined during Prohibition, referring to people who drank even though it was illegal, scoffing at the Volstead Act and its enforcers.

GOLF. Ade was an avid golfer.

Page 57

WORKING MEN'S EXCHANGE OR THE FARMERS' HOME. Generic urban and rural bar names. Chicago's infamous First

NOTES

Ward Alderman Michael "Hinky Dink" Kenna's saloon on Clark Street, south of Van Buren, was called the Workingman's Exchange. Kenna famously housed legions of down-and-out men in the Alaska Hotel above the bar, using them for their votes on Election Day.

GROGGERY. A lower-class bar.

Page 58

SAW-DUST PLACES. Working-class saloons covered their floors in sawdust so the wood shavings would absorb spilled alcohol, as well as spit and any other stray bodily fluids. Then the sawdust could be easily swept up.

TOM MORAN. The owner of a saloon on Randolph Street, near Chicago's courthouse. When he died in 1904, he merited a two-column obituary in the *Chicago Tribune*.

Page 61

DENNISON. A hotel bar in Indianapolis, frequented by local Republican politicians. Despite his Wet tendencies, Ade had long been an active Republican, the political party most firmly behind Prohibition (see McGirr for how this alignment shifted due to the repeal movement). In 1908, Republican presidential candidate William Howard Taft kicked off his campaign at Ade's Indiana estate. In 1932, Ade wrote a telegram to his US representative, William Wood (R IN 10), that shows the growing contradictions between being pro-repeal and a Republican:

WIRING [. . .] TO URGE YOU TO SIGN PETITION FOR GEN-
ERAL REFERENDUM ON PROHBITION WE ARE TRYING

TO REMAIN REPUBLICANS BUT MYSTIFIED AND AMAZED BY PERSISTENCE SOME PARTY MANAGERS WHO INSIST WHOLE MATTER OF REGULATING LIQUOR PROBLEMS IS SOLVED WHEREAS ANY OBSERVANT MAN CAN LOOK OUT OF ANY WINDOW AND GET CONCLUSIVE EVIDENCE THAT PROBLEM IS NOT SOLVED [. . .] WE BELIEVE THAT ANY LAWMAKER WET IN HIS HEART AND IN HIS STOM- ACH WHO PERSISTENTLY VOTES DRY THROUGH FEAR OF FANATICAL AND VENGEFUL PIOUS ELEMENT IS HIDING FROM DANGER WHICH NO LONGER EXISTS

Page 63

DR. SAMUEL JOHNSON. An eighteenth-century English man-of-letters, the author of the first *Dictionary of the English Language*, and a devotee of the saloon equivalents of his time. His biographer, James Boswell, quotes Johnson: "There is nothing which has yet been contrived by man, by which so much happiness is produced as by a good tavern or inn."

Page 69

ELEGANTINE. According to the *Oxford English Dictionary*, no such word exists. It is presumably a coinage of Ade's, for something pretentiously trying to be "elegant"; portmanteau with "elephantine," perhaps, to capture the outsized sense of self-importance some saloon keepers exhibited.

Page 70

PROHIBITION PARTY. Founded in 1869 and still in existence in 2016, the Prohibition Party is the third longest-lived political party in American history. Its animal avatar, parallel to the Republicans' elephant and the Democrats' donkey, is a camel. In the 2012 presidential election, 519 Americans cast votes for the Prohibition Party's candidate, Jack Fellure.

St. Vitus' Dance. A medieval European phenomenon of unknown origins, in which large groups of people would spasmodically dance in public. It is sometimes associated with extreme religious enthusiasms.

Page 76
"bit." A quarter-dollar is still sometimes known as "two bits."

Page 84
Park & Tilford. A famed grocery store in Harlem.

Jevne's. Charles Jevne was one of Chicago's first and most prosperous wholesale grocers.

Page 88
Mr. Emerson . . . Law of Compensation. In his *Essays: First Series* (1841), American transcendentalist Ralph Waldo Emerson argued that the doctrine of the Last Judgment—which insisted on eternal compensation in the next life, where the good would be rewarded and the evil punished—was flawed. To vastly oversimplify him, Emerson asserted that there was some good in evil people, and some evil in the good. This concept parallels Ade's rhetorical strategy of admitting to the evils of the saloon at its worst, while insisting, *contra* the Drys, that the saloon was not entirely a bad thing.

Page 90
any one who is not Prohibition has to be pro-saloon. With this wordplay, Ade mocks the Drys' slippery slope logic.

Guiteau, or Mr. Luetgert. Charles J. Guiteau assassinated President James Garfield in 1882. In 1897, Adolph Luetgert, a German immigrant to Chicago, was convicted of murdering his wife, Louise; he disposed of her body in a vat in his sausage factory, although he did not (as Chicago rumor and legend has had it) actually make her into sausage. See Loerzel.

Page 93

BRAKEMAN. Before the development of air pressure brakes, trains had to be stopped manually by workers stationed in each railcar. This strenuous labor made a brakeman, like a blacksmith, an epitome of masculine muscularity.

Page 94

FATHER MATHEW. Irish Roman Catholic priest and founder, in 1838, of the Cork Total Abstinence Society.

JOHN B. GOUGH. An English-born orator who promoted temperance from the United States to Britain, Ireland, and Europe.

WILLIAM JENNINGS BRYAN. Populist Democratic politician and renowned orator from Nebraska, best recalled today for his "Cross of Gold" speech against moneyed Eastern interests, in defense of Midwestern farmers and workers. A three-time Democratic candidate for president, Bryan was a vocal Dry, giving thousands of speeches in favor of Prohibition. Chicago's Revolution Brewing Company has named one of its delicious creations "Cross of Gold," an irony Bryan would probably find not to his taste.

"I NEVER DRINK BEHIND THE BAR." Song from Edward Harrigan's 1882 play, *The McSorleys*. The play references McSorley's Old Ale House, a New York institution since 1854.

NOTES

Page 95

"SNIT." An archaic term, still used in the Upper Midwest, for a small draft beer served as a chaser with hard liquor.

Page 96

"OTTO" . . . "MIKE" . . . "BILL." Stereotypical names for Germans, Irish, and nonimmigrant rural Americans (i.e., WASPs). Ade references some of the ethnic identities of many aspects of saloon culture but reflects little, if any, knowledge of urban immigrant neighborhood saloon culture, where the first language of the staff and patrons might be Polish, Czech, or Lithuanian rather than English. See Duis.

"ON THE HOUSE." Drys used "drinks on the house" to attack saloons, arguing that free drinks enticed workers to spend even more money. But it had a deeper meaning: buying a round made the bartender part of a community with his customers. Saloons were indeed "the poor man's club," and "club" didn't just mean the physical space. "To club" was to combine one's resources with others for the benefit of all. So the saloon wasn't just a semipublic place poor men could go; it was an informal institution where personal ties balanced other, more formal, relationships. When the barkeep bought a round for his customers, he symbolically joined their club, sharing customs, traditions, and values, rather than just commerce. See Powers.

Page 98

THE AUTHENTIC BAR-KEEP IS A THING OF THE PAST. Questionable now, but probably true in 1931. For more than a decade, any barkeep would have been, by definition, a lawbreaker working in an illegal business.

Page 99

CLUBS. Private clubs—where members pay for a shared space in which to dine, drink, network, and plot world (or local) domination in well-appointed semiprivacy—still survive into the twenty-first century but remain the domain of the well-to-do. The Chicago Athletic Association, once a hangout for Ade and many of his friends, is now a hotel with a public bar in what was once a private space. To view the opulent surroundings Ade once frequented, go to the Game Room on the second floor at 12 S. Michigan.

Page 100

THE SALOON WAS THE ROOSTER-CROW OF THE SPIRIT OF DE-MOCRACY. My favorite line in the whole book. Saloons were, and sometimes still can be, an ideal place for democratic ideals to flourish: open to anyone, accessible from the public street, convivial, a space where everything can be discussed. American independence was born in the taverns of East Coast seaboard towns, where American traitors (later known as "patriots") plotted sedition (later known as "the War of Independence") against the British. See Cheever.

BISHOP POTTER. According to the *Chicago Tribune*, at a meeting in 1899 to raise funds for a Temperance Saloon—with pool tables and food but no alcohol—Episcopal Bishop for New York Henry Codman Potter argued that conditions endured by the poor made the saloon necessary.

Page 101

THE HARNESS-SHOP. Whiskey or other drink would be informally sold or shared at small-town or big-city businesses.

NOTES

Page 104

BLUE-RIBBONERS. *The Blue Ribbon Official Gazette and Gospel Temperance Herald*'s stance on Prohibition is clear from its masthead.

Page 105

ROYSTERERS. Partiers; usually spelled "roisterers."

Page 106

DERELICT HANGERS-ON. While the "derelicts" he depicts here were certainly alcoholics, as much as they were created by the saloon, they were sustained there as well. Such men were not entirely social outcasts and would have been part of the community of their small town or urban neighborhood.

Page 107

DONNYBROOK. Slang for a brawl, from a Dublin neighborhood renowned for its annual fair and attendant binge-drinking, debauchery, and violence, probably involving hooligans.

Page 108

BLACK ALPACA. Dark woolen clothes, a typically dour temperance movement fashion statement.

"TEN NIGHTS IN A BAR-ROOM." *Ten Nights in a Bar-Room and What I Saw There* is an 1854 novel by T. S. Arthur, among the first temperance texts to call for legal Prohibition rather than just personal temperance or abstinence. Adapted into songs, plays, and films, some scholars credit it as the second-most popular nineteenth-century American novel, after Harriet Beecher Stowe's *Uncle Tom's Cabin*.

Page 110

CHARLEY CASE. A Vaudeville performer and songwriter. Vaudevillian comedy, attuned to the rough edges, language barriers, and quick pace of cities full of immigrants and workers looking for cheap and fast entertainment, emphasized slapstick and pratfalls. Think The Three Stooges, but with more ethnic jokes. Some historians credit Case with inventing stand-up comedy, the art of simply standing onstage to tell jokes in a monologue, without partners or props. Ade's mention of a "Salvation lassie" below (p. 112) refers to a song Case wrote, "There once was a poor young man who left his country home," the basis for W. C. Fields's 1933 film, *The Fatal Glass of Beer*. In that narrative, a teetotaler tricked into having one beer loses his mind (because one beer will do that to you) and breaks the tambourine of a female Salvation Army officer who had come into the saloon to save souls. She responds by reverting to her own pre-saved days and kicking him in the head.

MAURICE BARRYMORE. The founder of the Barrymore theatrical dynasty.

WILTON LACKAYE. An American stage and film actor who originated the role of Svengali.

Pages 110–111

"JIM" MCGARRY . . . "DOOLEY" PIECES BY "PETE" DUNNE. Finley Peter Dunne was "the first voice of genius" in Irish-American literature. A journalist who was a contemporary of Ade's, Dunne created Mr. Dooley, an Irish immigrant barkeep in Chicago's Bridgeport neighborhood, modeled on McGarry. Like Ade, Dooley worked in the American vernacular, but with an emphasis on the Irish voice and experience, while Ade's vernacular was more conventionally midwestern. See Fanning.

NOTES

Page 111

GEORGE SILVER. In 1907, the *Chicago Tribune* accused Silver of operating a dangerous dive bar, the Rialto, at Randolph and Clark Streets.

"BATH-HOUSE JOHN" COUGHLIN. The First Ward Alderman partner of "Hinky-Dink" Kenna (Chicago wards had two aldermen each until 1923) who was one of Chicago's most outrageously corrupt politicians.

GEORGE COHAN. An American vaudevillian, dancer, actor, singer, songwriter, composer, producer, and director, called "the man who owned Broadway." He is best remembered today for his patriotic compositions, "Over There," "A Yankee Doodle Dandy," and "A Grand Old Flag."

"HINKY-DINK" . . . WHOLESALE DEALER IN FLOATING VOTERS. First Ward Alderman Michael "Hinky-Dink" Kenna used tramps, hoboes, and vagrants to get votes.

Page 112

GRIZZLED HEROES OF 1861 TO 1865. Veterans of the American Civil War. The politics of the Civil War, and the living presence of many men who served on both sides, powerfully shaped the politics of late nineteenth–century America.

Page 113

ST. PATRICK'S DAY. Still an occasion for excessive celebration in American bars and heavily promoted by beer and liquor distributors, St. Patrick's Day exemplifies the sometimes comic fluidity of American identity in saloon culture. "Everyone's Irish" on St. Paddy's Day: if you define "Irish" as "wears a green plastic bowler hat and drinks too much for no good reason."

199

THE IRISH QUESTION. Not "Will you have another?" or "Why didn't James Joyce ever win a Nobel Prize?"; it is the politics of Ireland's relationship with Great Britain. Millions of poor and middle class Irish emigrated from their homeland, especially during and after the Potato Famine (or, in Irish, *An Gorta Mor*, "the Great Hunger") of 1845–52, and they brought their political concerns with them.

Page 114

SONS OF THE SOD. Irishmen, their descendants, or Celtic wannabes. "The old sod" is a sentimental term for Ireland.

"SHAMUS O'BRIEN." A lengthy narrative poem about the 1798 Irish Rebellion, by J. S. Le Fanu and published in 1850. It was popular in the United States well into the twentieth century but is now largely forgotten.

FREE SILVER. A complicated political and economic concern regarding federal monetary policy that drove much populist politics in the mid-nineteenth century. Restrictions on freely circulating money were thought to favor the wealthy over farmers and other workers.

FENIAN. An Irish rebel, or separatist, especially from the failed rising of 1867. The Fenian Brotherhood was an Irish-American secret society that sought to fund rebellion in Ireland.

TOM HEATH, OF MCINTYRE AND HEATH. Heath and James McIntyre were blackface vaudevillians.

ORANGEADE. Orange is the color associated with Irish Protestantism and opposition to Irish independence.

NOTES

"TOM AND JERRY." A hot mixed drink, with various recipes, including the one here.

Page 115
WHATEVER IS THE PLURAL OF TOM AND JERRY. Nelson Algren suggests "Tom and Jerries."

Page 116
ATMOSPHERE THAT YOU COULD CUT WITH A KNIFE. Besides the smells of the alcohol and the food and the perhaps-rarely-bathed clientele, smoking was not regulated in any way. Many an ill-ventilated saloon would have had an atmosphere that would now seem to be composed primarily of semisolid carcinogens.

LIKE THE GREEN BAY TREE. Psalms 37:35: "I have seen the wicked in great power, and spreading himself like a green bay tree." This is an ambiguous Biblical verse for Ade's purposes, in that it seems to imply that the powers-that-be in saloons were wicked.

GAMBRINUS. One of those legendary European characters, like Santa Claus, who has certain attributes but takes different forms in different nations. Not a god, not a saint, not a historic figure, Gambrinus is a legendary embodiment of brewing beer and its subsequent good fellowship. The "Gambrinus in overalls" here would be the delivery driver for the local brewery.

Page 117
TRADITIONS AND CUSTOMS WERE BASED ON THE BROAD-MINDED ASSUMPTION THAT ONE MAN WAS JUST AS GOOD AS ANOTHER, AND POSSIBLY BETTER. One definition of American democracy manifested in saloon culture.

Page 118

Songs mentioned here can be found with an Internet search. Some have ethnic/immigrant roots, others are folk music or Tin Pan Alley compositions. The old-time saloon predated most mechanical methods of reproducing music. Communal sing-alongs have been replaced by jukeboxes, DJs, or bartenders' iPods, but music is still one *raison d'etre* for public drinking spaces, even if they are not live music venues. The widespread evil of karaoke I will not remark upon.

Page 119

LACHRYMOSE PERIOD. Presumably a coinage of Ade's, emphasizing the tearful sentimentality of many songs sung in saloons.

Page 120

SÄNGERFEST. German singing party.

UNDERTAKING PARLORS OR THE MOLASSES FACTORY. Songs were either overly obsessed with death or overly sweet.

Page 123

AL JOLSON. A blackface vaudevillian and star of the first talking motion picture, *The Jazz Singer*. "Mammy" was his signature tune.

Page 129

WILLIE AND EUGENE HOWARD. German-born Jewish brothers who performed in burlesque, vaudeville, film, and radio for decades.

BOBBY BURNS. Scottish poet Robert Burns, whose "Auld Lang Syne" might be the poem most often recited (or sung) in bars to this day, but only on two days: New Year's Eve and his birthday, January 25, celebrated as "Burnsday."

NOTES

Page 130

"THE FACE ON THE BAR-ROOM FLOOR." Sentimental ballad of 1897 by Hugh Antoine D'Arcy, based on an 1872 poem by John Henry Titus, and the basis for a 1914 film by Charlie Chaplin. It depicts the tearful death of an artist who lost his one true love; he tells his story in exchange for drinks, before dropping dead of a broken heart after drawing her face on the barroom floor.

Page 131

NEWHALL HOUSE. A hotel in Milwaukee that burned down in 1883, with seventy-one of some three hundred guests perishing.

Page 134

TOM THUMB. A little-person showman famed for his performances in Barnum and Bailey's Circus. Along with his wife, he survived the Newhall House hotel fire.

DORNICKS. Small stones.

Page 135

GOTHENBERG PLAN OF SWEDEN. A government monopoly on liquor sales. A few US states (and most Canadian provinces) later adopted this approach.

Page 137

BEER-DRINKING BECAME POPULAR . . . SCHLITZ . . . BUSCH . . . LEMP. Twenty-first-century craft breweries feature India pale ales and other complex brews, but since the repeal, lager beer (especially in its macrobrew varieties) has, for better or worse, been considered the American beer style. Yet from the time of the Pilgrims until the 1840s, Americans drank English-style ales. Then German immigrants brought the technology and expertise to brew lagers, but it took them some time to win over American tastes and overcome prejudice. Among Nativists, the key Dry constituency, "Irish Whiskey and German Lager" were shorthand for evils brought to the United States by immigrants. The brewers named here were all German ethnics whose conflicted loyalties in the years leading up to the Great War contributed to the Drys' depiction of lager as un-American. These breweries were huge forces in the American economy and innovators in technology, shipping, and marketing. Some survive to this day, while others were obliterated by Prohibition. See Okrent.

ENGLISH SYNDICATE. Not an illegal criminal syndicate, but an investment group. See Skilnik.

Page 141

"MADE MILWAUKEE FAMOUS." The act that first made Schlitz, and Milwaukee, famous was their response to Chicago's Great Fire of 1871; trains and boatloads of beer arrived to quench the thirst of Chicagoans whose own breweries were smoldering cinders. For decades thereafter, Chicagoans toasted Milwaukee for its generosity.

OPEN THEIR OWN PLACES. Known as "tied houses," such saloons were owned outright by breweries, and the men who ran the bars had no goal other than to sell as much beer as possible, regardless of the law. In Chicago, several buildings that were once Schlitz-owned tied houses still stand, with their characteristic cream-colored brick and Schlitz Globe logo in terra cotta. The best preserved is perhaps the bar and music venue Schuba's, at Belmont and Southport.

Page 144

Boys of high-school age were permitted to line up at the bar and little children brought in cans to be filled. Many saloon owners disregarded restrictions on drinking age, among other laws, and so Dry propaganda depicted all saloons as lawless and disreputable.

"Wot't'ell?" "What the hell?" A flippant attitude towards potential consequences of flouting the law, as well as slurred speech that suggests the barkeep here quoted has imbibed more than a few snits.

"harness bull." A police officer who walks a regular route in a neighborhood, or a beat cop. But more particularly, one who's been paid off and so works for the criminals, as a domestic animal works for a farmer.

a square guy. Standards of honesty ("being square" not in the sense of being not-hip, but in the sense of being reliable, like a carpenter's square) are applied even with graft and vice. An honest grafter is one who, when bought, stays bought. See Powers.

Page 149

Damon and Pythias. In Greek mythology, exemplars of devoted male friendship.

"pizen." Poison, as pronounced in one Irish accent.

Page 152

a certain kind of noisy braggart. This epic poetic vernacular language recalls a piece by Mark Twain. (Ade cofounded Chicago's Mark Twain Society.) In the manuscript of *Adventures of Huckleberry Finn*, chapter XVI depicts Huck sneaking onto a raft and overhearing two raftsmen build up to a potential fistfight. While Bud in Ade's saloon is "the ory boryalis," willing to fight anyone in the place, one of Twain's raftsmen claims, "I scratch my head with the lightning and purr myself to sleep with the thunder! When I'm cold I bile the Gulf of Mexico and bathe in it." His opponent claims that he was "sired by a hurricane, dam'd by an earthquake, half-brother to the cholera, nearly related to the smallpox on the mother's side." Twain published the passage in *Life on the Mississippi* in 1883 before the publication of *Huck Finn*; he later cut it, and so it is not included in most editions of the novel. See Blair and Fischer's edition of Twain.

FRANK AND JESSE JAMES . . . "WILD BILL" HICKOCK. Iconic outlaws of the American West who are folk heroes because they challenged powerful institutions like railroads and banks.

Page 154

JOHN BARLEYCORN. Personification of the evils of drink for Drys; originally from English and Scottish folk ballads dating back to the Middle Ages, which decried the sway of drink while celebrating its healing powers. Jack London entitled his 1913 autobiography dealing with his struggle with the bottle *John Barleycorn*.

Page 155

SHOOING THE WOLF. During the Great Depression, Wets thought that people had more to worry about than whether other people drank. "The wolf at the door" has long been an image of economic privation.

Page 156

DOGGERIES. Low-class bars.

NOTES

Page 159

THE COCKTAIL. Cocktail aficionados attempted to preserve drink recipes even during Prohibition. Books like *The Saloon in the Home* mocked the Drys by including quotations from temperance literature interleaved with recipes for cocktails. *Tom and Jerry's Bartender's Guide* and *The Barkeeper's Manual*, among countless other books, were published in 1934 after the repeal. Today, a craft cocktail bar culture thrives in cities across the United States, as some bartenders have come to think of themselves as chefs who just happen to work with liquids, revising old drinks and inventing new ones.

Page 160

RATHSKELLERS. German bars.

BLANKET DAILIES. Broadsheet newspapers; so called because their large size enabled homeless people sleeping in public, say on park benches, to use them as blankets.

"SPEAK-EASIES." A "speak-easy" was, of course, an illegal bar during Prohibition. The source of the term is much contested, but many illegal bars operated in private homes or small commercial spaces. Noise complaints might bring the attention of the law, so staff would tell customers to be quiet, or "speak easy." See Okrent; McGirr.

BILL ROGERS. Will Rogers, popular and populist American comedian. Ade here quotes one of Rogers's most famed one-liners.

DUN AND BRADSTREET. Commercial report that provides insider information to investors, renowned for its broad and comprehensive research into corporate histories.

Page 162

SHOT-GUN MARRIAGES. Marriages imposed on the groom, by force of the bride's family's shotgun, presumably because the bride had been impregnated.

Page 164

ROUNDERS. Drunks; probably from people who buy rounds in a saloon.

Pages 164–165

22ND STREET . . . SOUTH ON HALSTED STREET. This route would lead to the Chicago Stock Yards and its associated slaughterhouses.

Page 165

GEORGE PRIMROSE. Vaudeville performer who began his career as a blackface minstrel.

BOB COLE . . . AND JOHNSON. Composer, actor, and producer, Cole is credited by some historians with writing, in 1897, the first African American musical, *A Trip to Coontown*. He and his African American partners, the Johnson brothers, helped pave the way to mainstream success for later black performers, and he wrote criticism of the use of racial and racist stereotypes in African American (as well as mainstream white) drama. Famed blues genius W. C. Handy wrote the music for the song.

Page 168

LEGALIZE ANY KIND OF DRINKING. Such slippery slope arguments once made against the repeal parallel those made now against the legalization of marijuana. The logic of Prohibition, once in place, is difficult to budge. See McGirr.

NOTES

Page 169

THEY SHOULD REMEMBER THAT THE AMERICAN PUBLIC WILL NOT STAND FOR INTOLERANCE. One can only hope.

Page 171

ROCKEFELLERS ... CANDLER. American millionaires who contributed vast sums of money to the Dry cause.

Page 172

COL. "JIM HAM" LEWIS. James Hamilton Lewis, Democratic senator from Illinois from 1913 to 1919 and from 1931 to 1939. He was a renowned eccentric and devoted Wet.

Page 174

TURN HIM LOOSE AGAIN? This odd conclusion suggests Ade was sincere in not wanting a return to the wide-open saloons of old, and it gives him some cover for his claim that this volume is "not Wet—not Dry, just history." However, the illustration on the facing page and its caption—the final words of the text— undercuts this purported neutrality: "Oh, Yes?" The image of a respectable and smiling barkeep speaking to a customer suggests that Americans would indeed welcome the rebirth of saloons, so long as there were fewer barrelhouses or doggeries and more respectable or elegant resorts.

And they got their wish. Late in the afternoon of December 5, 1933, the Twenty-First Amendment to the US Constitution was ratified by Utah, and national Prohibition came to an end. Many states, counties, and municipalities used the local option to remain dry; others enacted laws to regulate public drinking in order to ensure that the commercial and criminal excesses of the old-time saloon would not return. The Twenty-First Amendment was the only amendment to repeal another, and the only one ever ratified by specially called State Constitutional Conventions, rather than by state legislatures. The Eighteenth Amendment had been the first with a deadline for its passing; many Wet politicians who voted Dry out of fear of the Anti-Saloon League believed that the seven-year deadline would prevent Prohibition from ever being enacted. Instead, to their shock and dismay, it took just under thirteen months.

Some fourteen years later, to the undying consternation of the Drys, the repeal took eight months and thirteen days.

Cheers.

BIBLIOGRAPHY

George Ade's books are almost all out of print. Collections of Ade's papers reside at the Newberry Library of Chicago (my source for anything referencing his papers) and the Purdue University Library. No full-length biography of Ade (1866– 1944) is in print, but a brief one can be found at the Purdue Library website. For the portrait of Ade from Chapin and Gore's saloon, visit http://blog.chicagohistory.org/index.php /2011/03/caricature-of-ade-and-wells-1912/.

The source for any note which references the *Chicago Tribune* can be found with an Internet search using the subject's name and the newspaper archive. Any note regarding song lyrics can also be tracked down online; space limitations prevent both full-scale analysis of the lyrics and complete references to each and every songwriter or composer. The Library of Congress's National Jukebox is an essential source as well.

BIBLIOGRAPHY

The five books that anyone interested in this period of American history should read, and my main sources, are:

Duis, Perry. *The Saloon: Public Drinking in Chicago and Boston, 1880–1920*. Chicago: University of Illinois Press, 1983.

McGirr, Lisa. *The War on Alcohol: Prohibition and the Rise of the American State*. New York: Norton, 2016.

Okrent, Daniel. *Last Call: The Rise and Fall of Prohibition*. New York: Scribner, 2010.

Powers, Madelon. *Faces along the Bar: Lore and Order in the Working Man's Saloon, 1870–1920*. Chicago: University of Chicago Press, 1998.

Skilnik, Bob. *Beer: A History of Brewing in Chicago*. Fort Lee, NJ: Barricade Books, 2006.

Other texts consulted or referenced:

Ade Papers. Newberry Library, Chicago.

Algren, Nelson. *Chicago: City on the Make*. 1951. Annotated edition, edited by David Schmittgens and Bill Savage. Chicago: University of Chicago Press, 2011.

Arthur, T. S. *Ten Nights in a Bar-Room, and What I Saw There*. Boston: L. P. Crown, 1854.

The Barkeeper's Manual of 1910: The Art of Mixing. N.p.: Pierce and Hebner, 1934.

Boswell, James. *The Life of Samuel Johnson, LL.D.* 1791.

Cheever, Susan. *Drinking in America: Our Secret History*. New York: Twelve, 2015.

Dunbar, Robin, et al. "Friends on Tap: The Role of Pubs at the Heart of the Community. A Report for CAMRA." Department of Experimental Psychology, University of Oxford. 2016.

Eig, Jonathan. *Get Capone: The Secret Plot that Captured America's Most Wanted Gangster*. New York: Simon and Schuster, 2010.

Fanning, Charles. *Finley Peter Dunne and Mr. Dooley: The Chicago Years*. Lexington: University Press of Kentucky, 1978.

Kelly, Fred C. *George Ade: Warmhearted Satirist.* New York: Bobbs-Merrill, 1947.

Loerzel, Robert. *The Alchemy of Bones: Chicago's Luetgert Murder Case of 1897.* Chicago: University of Illinois Press, 2003.

Oldenburg, Ray. *The Great Good Place: Cafes, Coffee Shops, Bookstores, Bars, Hair Salons, and Other Hangouts at the Heart of a Community.* New York: Paragon Books, 1989.

Tafoya, Eddie. *The Legacy of the Wisecrack: Stand-up Comedy as the Great American Literary Form.* Boca Raton, FL: Brown, Walker Press, 2009.

Tom and Jerry's Bartender's Guide: How to Mix Drinks. Pre-Prohibitions Recipes. Chicago: Charles T. Powner, 1934.

Twain, Mark. *Adventures of Huckleberry Finn.* Edited by Walter Blair and Victor Fischer. Berkeley: University of California Press, 1985.

Wilson, Samuel Paynter. *Chicago and Its Cess-Pools of Infamy.* N.p., [1915?].

ACKNOWLEDGEMENTS

Chicago boasts an amazing array of historians, critics, scholars, and writers who are knowledgeable, opinionated, and—most of all—generous with their time and expertise. Lots of people helped me with this book, and they know who they are: the kind of people who'd rather see more notes and less space spent listing their names.

ABOUT THE EDITOR / ANNOTATOR

Bill Savage is an Associate Professor of Instruction in the English Department at Northwestern University. At the Newberry Library of Chicago, he leads a seminar entitled "The City that Drinks: Saloon History and Culture in Chicago Literature and Film." He also worked as a bartender for over thirty years.